# FINDING MY
# VOICE

# FINDING MY VOICE

## THE PETER BROCKLEHURST STORY

**Peter Brocklehurst**
**with Debbie Bennett**

ALLEN&UNWIN

*Back cover (from top to bottom)*: Peter with Steve Waugh; with José Carreras (photo by Bill Green at Sony); with Bob Carr, Premier of New South Wales; with Kerri-Anne Kennerley; with Alan Jones and Vladimir Vais; and with Kate Ceberano.

First published in Australia in 2004 by Allen & Unwin

Allen & Unwin
83 Alexander Street
Crows Nest NSW 2065
Australia
Phone:   (61 2) 8425 0100
Fax:     (61 2) 9906 2218
Email:   info@allenandunwin.com
Web:     www.allenandunwin.com

National Library of Australia
Cataloguing-in-Publication entry:

Brocklehurst, Peter, 1959– .
  Finding my voice.

  ISBN 1 74114 344 6.

  1. Brocklehurst, Peter, 1959– . 2. Singers – Australia –
  Biography. I. Title.

782.0092

Typeset in 12.5/16.7 pt Bembo by Midland Typesetters, Maryborough, Victoria
Printed by Griffin Press, Netley, South Australia

10 9 8 7 6 5 4 3 2 1

# FOREWORD

My parents were refugees from war-torn Europe who fled to Australia with dreams of creating a wonderful new life filled with opportunities for themselves and their only infant son. Thus, as I sat opposite Peter Brocklehurst for the very first time in February 2002, having lunch in that Hawthorn pub and listening to an abbreviated version of his very complex life, initially the most compelling part of his story was of his migrant parents who had struggled through unimaginable adversities to rear a strong, if somewhat disjointed family.

I was listening to the most far-fetched tales of survival imaginable. How did these people do it? What drives two basically uneducated, unskilled people to travel from the top of our planet to near its bottom in search of answers to their dreams? What encourages them to produce eight children, then suffer extreme hardships trying to rear them? I was hearing tales of parental love and support yet, anomalously, these stories were also filled with horrific poverty, hunger and hopelessness.

My parents also each worked several jobs. But for them it was to give their child a proper education and to endeavour to break down the social barriers of a very bigoted, rather unsophisticated yet evolving 1950s Australia. They knew that if I were to have any chance of fulfilling whatever promise or talent I might have, first and foremost I had to have a good education. So I kept thinking, why did Peter's parents place so little emphasis on educating their offspring?

I couldn't help but like the guy telling the stories! He was pleasant looking, with an open, cheerful face, a really cheeky grin and a mischievous sense of humour. He seemed intelligent enough. He sounded happy enough. He appeared to be a little nervous but still purveyed relevant information in a clear and coherent way.

My dad chain-smoked because he was dissatisfied with his achievements, and eventually became desperately depressed. Peter told of a similar habit but omitted the punchline. There was much more here than met the eye.

Incongruously, as Peter kept up this façade of contentment, he spoke honestly about his broken heart, his shattered dreams, his apparent talent. Apparent only because scores of people had lauded it exultantly but no one had ever committed to its development. Some, he claimed, had even described his tenor voice as the best in the world.

To be totally honest it all seemed a bit far-fetched. A gypsy upbringing, a grade five education, twenty years of cigarettes, drugs and rock'n'roll, a day job as a shoe repairer, all leading inexorably towards a spiritually joyous ending on the stage as the world's greatest tenor. My mind couldn't quite seriously absorb this scenario.

But by nature I am a dreamer with a gambler's optimistic spirit. Peter's story had aroused both these characteristics. I sensed that if what I was hearing was indeed factual then the most incredible journey lay ahead. The sceptical one-time journalist in me needed to know more. The romantic dreamer was hankering for the challenge.

Peter had mentioned two mentors—a Russian-born maestro named Vladimir Vais and a Canadian-born voice coach, Stephen Grant. The former had been conductor at the fabled Bolshoi Theatre in Moscow for eleven years and had even accompanied the legendary Rudolph Nureyev on his last tour.

Over the next week I arranged to meet with each of these men, who have continued to be so important in Peter's evolution, and resolved to ask one simple question: 'How would you rate Peter Brocklehurst on a world scale?'

The maestro replied, 'He's golden. A voice like this comes once in a hundred years. In my life there have been two great tenors—Franco Corelli and Peter Brocklehurst.'

Stephen Grant was far more succinct: 'His voice is ten out of ten. But as yet he knows nothing.'

Something very unusual occurred inside me that day. I knew categorically that I couldn't allow Peter to endure that cramped, filthy bootshop any longer. I just had to get him out of there, away from the epoxy resins and glues he was inhaling daily. Somehow I had to find a path for him to the great concert halls of the world. His talent had to be liberated and reach its potential.

There were still many unanswered questions as to how

this could be achieved. After all, we were very different human beings from backgrounds which socially could not have been farther apart. Could such an odd couple survive? And what if the project failed and Peter was once more dumped, battered and rejected, back to where I had found him? Could he psychologically hack such a mammoth let-down?

But perhaps the major of many negatives was that I knew absolutely nix about the music business. To this day I cannot actually say what compelled me to decide we should have a go. Perhaps the challenge, maybe the story, but most likely it just felt right.

It has been a truly amazing journey for us all. Peter has been an inspiration. He promised 100 per cent dedication. He has given 110 per cent. Never have I seen anyone immerse themselves so completely in a challenge. Each day he grows in stature as a performer but mostly he has risen to astounding levels of character and charisma as a person. Indeed, I believe that watching him evolve has transformed and inspired me to be a better person. I have learned an extraordinary amount about the human spirit from him.

I have shared his first 'plane ride as an adult'. I have shared his anxiety over his premier solo classical perform-ance. I have shared his struggle to overcome nerves for media interviews. I have shared his elation upon signing his global record contract with Sony Music. I have witnessed his exhaustion after singing relentlessly to a live phil-harmonic orchestra to complete his first CD album within the four-day deadline. I have shared his elation when *Boots and All* debuted as the No.1 classical album nationally. But above all I have shared his dream to give unreserved pleasure to all those who listen to his music.

Peter's favourite saying is, 'If I have touched someone or given them pleasure then I am a success.' Well, I can happily say to Peter that he has touched me and my family and many of our friends and relatives in a myriad positive ways.

As a racehorse owner I have been fortunate enough to win some nice events. I know well the tense, clammy state of anticipation when awaiting the start of a race. Well, that's but a trifle compared to waiting for Peter to start a performance. And collecting a Caulfield Cup or a Golden Slipper is truly insignificant when weighed up against the joy on Peter's face when his audiences inevitably erupt in rapturous applause.

The story you are about to read is so raw and con-fronting, in fact so inspiring and uplifting in nature, and so incredible that it will only be at its end that you will fully understand why this journey is so wondrous. But please remember it is only a work in progress, with my estimation being that at least 80 per cent of Peter's life story is left for the future to unveil. We won't stop until La Scala, Covent Garden, Carnegie Hall, the Metropolitan and the Sydney Opera House, among a score of other great arenas, have been 'scaled' and conquered.

God bless you Peter, I know you will do it.

*Nick Columb*

# Contents

Foreword by Nick Columb                                   5

1    'Ladies and gentlemen . . .'                        15
2    Darwin in the late 1960s                            27
3    Dad told me he counted 79 moves                     43
4    The rest of the family piled into the car           63
5    This time it was different                          81
6    'A whirlwind romance' . . .                         91
7    Once again I was on the road                       103
8    There is a distinct and busy band scene            121
9    I had no trouble getting gigs                      131
10   Sharon was still working                           143
11   I was a married man with three children            161
12   It was a strange feeling being single              171
13   It took me a few days to find the courage          181
14   Those with an eye for a racehorse                  199
15   It is now late 2003                                217

Acknowledgements                                        227

A very special, heartfelt thank you to my 'ghost', Debbie Bennett. A difficult and traumatic journey was made easier as, together, we revisited memories of the past. This book would not have been possible were it not for the special relationship of trust and affinity we developed. Thank you.

## CHAPTER 1

## 'LADIES AND GENTLEMEN . . .'

Eddie Maguire's voice echoed throughout the cavernous auditorium, commanding silence from the crowd. I too stood silent, nervously fingering the buttons of the unfamiliar starched white shirt, wondering whether my collar was straight, whether my eyes or in fact my whole body disclosed the mild terror that was churning around inside me.

'It is my pleasure', the voice continued, 'to present to you one of the greatest tenors in the world . . . Mr Peter Brocklehurst!'

Eddie finished his introduction and looked across the stage to where I stood. Melbourne's Telstra Dome rumbled with the sound of applause. *One of the greatest tenors in the world.*

It was me. I was the one he was talking about with those eight words—eight wonderful words that lifted me to heights beyond my wildest dreams.

I was the main act in a night celebrating the career of one of Australia's most revered sporting heroes, AFL football legend Ron Barassi. Maestro Vladimir Vais and renowned songwriter Mike Brady had written a song especially for me, and I was to sing it to commemorate Ron's career.

The applause continued as I walked to centre stage and looked out at the audience. The cream of Australia's sporting and social elite looked back at me.

Not for the first time, I wondered who they saw as they stared expectantly up at the stage. A year ago, I would have been looking up at them as I mended their expensive footwear in my shoe-repair shop in Hawthorn. Then I was a cobbler who happened to be a singer. Now I was sharing with them the talent I had been blessed with. I was living my dream, my life's ambition. In just a handful of months, I had evolved from just some guy who *liked* to sing opera into a performing tenor surrounded by a group of advisers and new-found friends, a film crew following my every move.

A tenor is what and who I am. Singing is my future and for nearly as long as I can remember it has been an integral part of my past.

If I had to use one word to describe my life it would be 'undulating'. It seems appropriate because of all the ups and downs that have been part of it: the times of real happiness but also the times of fear, loneliness and despair. These are the moments and episodes I remember, the experiences I have carried with me throughout my life that have shaped the person I have become.

I often tell people that I grew up in the back of a station wagon. Perhaps not literally, but when I think of home, of the four walls that for most people would hold familiar memories, for me it is an old, smoke-filled station wagon that springs to mind—the car that took our family and everything we owned from place to place in many parts of Australia.

My memories of being in the car and travelling aren't linked to leaving any particular place or arriving at a particular destination. Most people get in their car to go home, but for me it often seemed that we went from a house to home—the car was my home.

'Are we there yet?' How often did those words echo around the car in my childhood? Finally, one journey is over and today I find myself taking a completely different and unfamiliar road.

But as I stand looking out at the sea of faces waiting for me to sing, I know that the question remains the same. *Are we there yet?*

Tom and Helen Brocklehurst met at a dance in Yorkshire, England in the mid 1950s, when she was just seventeen and he was nineteen. Both had led typical post-war working-class lives, leaving school early to join the ranks of the workforce. Mum had worked in factories and as a domestic in the homes of the wealthy, while Dad became a coalminer at the age of fourteen before joining the army.

Neither would have had any illusions about the life they chose when they took the decision to marry young. But they were in love, so much so that Dad was actually kicked out of the army because he kept going AWOL to visit Mum. Mum was a real stunner in her younger days, so I think Dad was smitten, and Mum must have been pretty taken with Dad in his lance corporal's uniform, too.

Not long after they married, my older brother Paul was born. So they probably thought they knew what to expect a few years later when, on 23 October 1959, Mum went into labour with me.

The family was living in one of the tiny houses that lined the streets of working-class suburbs throughout England—rows and rows of grey featureless buildings whose front doors opened directly onto the footpath. Lines of homes where the human drama and struggle to survive was played out behind those closed doors.

As was the custom in those days, the midwife was called to the house as Mum entered the last stages of labour. Dad and Nan, my Mum's mum, were banished downstairs as my arrival became imminent.

Dad smoked as he paced up and down. He kept telling himself there was nothing to worry about, but couldn't shake the feeling of unease and guilt most husbands feel as their wives go through the agony of giving birth.

Finally the screams and sounds of labour coming from the bedroom stopped and Dad and Nan looked at each other with a mixture of relief and joy. It was over, the baby had arrived. But in the same instant, they both realised that something was wrong. The house was too quiet; there was no high-pitched, indignant squall of a newborn.

The door of the bedroom opened and the midwife came downstairs and looked at both of them. With abrupt sympathy she said, 'He didn't make it. He's dead.'

My Nan was a tiny woman, but what she lacked in stature she made up for in heart, particularly where her family was concerned. Raising herself to her full height, she glared up at the midwife and said, 'Like bloody hell he is. He was kicking just five minutes ago.' Bustling up the stairs towards the bedroom, she gave the midwife a look that would stop a charging bull as she yelled to Dad to bring her a bucket of cold water and a bucket of hot. (That's obviously why they boil water in the movies!)

Nan rushed into the room where Mum had been left lying alone and distraught. Ignoring her, she grabbed my lifeless body from the corner where I had been laid on the floor, wrapped in a blanket ready for burial. Holding me by my feet, she dunked me head first into the hot water, then into the cold, before whacking me on the back. And that was the first time my voice was heard. A piercing yell that announced to the world that I was very much alive.

This story has become part of the folklore of our family, one of those tales that grows with each retelling. As it is with most people, a lot of my own memories of childhood are disjointed and out of sequence, mixed with stories I have been told and experiences I have lived. There are times I remember vividly and times I have forgotten altogether.

I can remember slipping in the snow on the way to the outside toilet, so that must have been in England. And I have vague but valuable memories of the time we spent with Dad's parents. His Mum worked in a factory that made liquorice allsorts, and whenever we went to visit she would reach into a box she kept on top of a cupboard and fill our cupped hands with the most delicious-smelling liquorice. Perhaps I have romanticised the sensation but I have never tasted nor smelt liquorice like that since. Lollies, or sweets as they were called in England, were not an everyday thing for us, so holding a handful of liquorice was like being given gold. As we never got to know Dad's parents well, it is important to me that my few recollections are happy.

Even in England, our family moved around a lot. It was more Mum who had the gypsy in her soul, she always seemed to be searching for somewhere or something new. That's probably what led us to Australia in the first place.

The drama of my birth didn't seem to deter Mum and Dad from having more children. My sister Mandy was born about two years later, to be followed over the years by Josie, Sarah, Jamie, Tommy and Rebecca. So I suppose that life in Australia at least offered the family a chance of a way out, an opportunity that few working-class people in England would ever have.

I do have a clear recollection of the day we left to come to Australia as ten-pound Poms. (Under Australia's immigration program, that's what it cost each of our parents to travel. Children travelled free.) We stood in front of the huge Qantas plane that was to take us to the other side of the world and I knew that there was no way that huge thing would stay in the air, it just didn't make sense. With all the determination I could muster, I turned to my father and said, 'I'm not getting in that blooming thing!' The logic I used as a five-year-old has stayed with me to this day, and I still feel a slight unease when flying around the country.

Needless to say, I did get on the plane and we landed at Mascot Airport in Sydney on 19 April 1965, a year after the Beatles descended on the colonies with the 'British Music Invasion'. A lot less fanfare greeted our arrival. Like thousands of other migrant families, we arrived with little more than hope and the expectation of a better life.

Not long after we arrived Dad bought an EK Holden station wagon and our life on the road began. Of course this was in those lovely innocent days before we knew about the dangers of smoking or road trauma. Looking back, we could have been the poster family for many of today's safety campaigns—the how-not-to pictures.

Both Mum and Dad were heavy smokers and, with the windows up, the car was like a smoke bubble hurtling along the roads. My granddad had shown Dad the basics of how to drive, but he didn't bother getting his licence for years, and most of the cars he owned were unregistered. We would all squash in wherever there was space—seatbelts were unheard of—and with all our stuff packed around us we would head off for the next destination. A lot of the roads we took in those days weren't sealed, but we always managed to get to where we were going.

For us the car became home, the place where we were familiar with the smell and the rhythm of the road and we were safe because we had each other. The structure of our home wasn't bricks and mortar; it was the love that held us together. Love and family were the constants in our lives.

Mum's parents and my aunt and uncle had come to Sydney before us, so we stayed with them for a while before moving on . . . three months in Manly, three months in Narrabeen, three months in Gosford, and so on. Along the way we would camp or stay at caravan parks. Sarah was born in Gosford, and then we moved on to Pearl Beach, where we lived for a while in a house.

Always moving on, friendships broken before they had really begun, the look of places and the faces of people merging into each other as time passed by. Staying in houses, caravans, tents, or even sleeping on the side of road, with the girls in the car and the boys outside, sheltered under a makeshift tarpaulin—after Dad had cooked us supper on a campfire with the vegies we'd picked from crops along the road. Then there were the times Mum would plant a garden at one of the houses, hoping to pick our own vegies, only to find we were on the move again before they ripened. Most of all, though, there were the endless meals of fish and chips from roadside cafes.

We kids would escape the cramped confines of the car as soon as we stopped, tumbling out and eager to explore a new place. Freed from the smoke and the press of bodies, I would grab the chance of getting away from it all for a while by running as far and as fast as I could until I had to turn round and head back, exhausted but elated to be back with the family.

The faces and voices of most of the people we met along the way have been lost to time. But there are some I will never forget, no matter how hard I try.

When my little sister Mandy and I were very young—I was seven and Mandy about five-and-a-half or six—we were abducted by a paedophile who abused us and kept us locked in his car for days. We were living in Terrigal, north of Sydney, at the time. It was a horrifying experience that was just too big, too bad for any of us to deal with. When it was over, we coped the best way we could. We pushed what had happened away from us, letting it rest in the subconscious of our family's memory. We moved as far away as possible, both physically and emotionally.

I was too little then to truly understand the enormity of

what had happened to me, but it was something that will never leave me. As a grown man, I have come to learn that you can never run from what is deep inside you. Some things are never truly gone; they lie within you ready to emerge when you are at your most vulnerable.

As a child growing up, the experience was gradually pushed away from my reality. But it remained part of me and played an integral part in what I was becoming as a person. Naturally, I neither knew nor understood any of this at the time. While the physical memory might be a little dimmer these days, the effect is still just as strong. To discuss what happened within the context of my childhood would imply a far greater insight than I had at the time. So, in the same way as I had to in my adult life, I will return to that experience and everything it meant to me later.

Mum's parents had moved on to Darwin with my aunt and uncle, and after the abduction we packed up the car and headed off to join them. The start of the trip was different to the other times; there was a lot of silence and a lot of pain. No one spoke about what had happened, not even Mandy or me, but as we travelled things seemed to return to normal. We started singing—'Summer Holiday' and 'Chitty Chitty Bang Bang' are two I remember—and the car gradually became a safe place for us again.

I always loved it when we drove at night. I would drift in and out of sleep while staring up at the stars. It enhanced the security I felt inside the car to gaze at the blackest of skies dotted with brilliant, bright points of light millions of miles away. Unlike us down on earth, the stars never seemed to move. Perhaps in their certainty they became like an anchor as we hurtled along the dusty roads.

I'm fairly sure it was on the trip to Darwin that we came across the strangest phenomenon I have ever seen. We were driving at night when Dad pulled the car over. We were all dozing but must have woken when the rhythm of the car stopped. It was then that we saw what looked like basketballs bouncing around in front of us. Only these basketballs were glowing. We had no idea what it was we were seeing and, if it was just me, I would have thought I was having a weird dream. But if I was dreaming, then the whole family was sharing my dream.

We sat there for what seemed like ages and I can remember thinking these were little stars that had fallen from the sky. For some reason I wasn't scared. Perhaps it was just that I was a little boy and, in spite of what had happened in Terrigal just a few weeks before, a part of me still wanted to believe in magic. Or maybe it was that I knew I was safe because I was in the car with my family. Whatever it was, I know it felt special to be part of something so mysterious.

Much later, when we arrived in Darwin, Granddad told us we had been lucky enough to see what many considered to be an Aboriginal myth—the *min min* lights. No one is really sure what causes them. I'm sure scientists have tried to come up with a good explanation—possibly refracted light rays from a star just below the horizon or maybe escaping gas if seen over marshy areas—but apparently they are seen so rarely that many people doubt they even exist.

Our first home in Darwin was a dusty, flat caravan park on the main road. We lived there while we were waiting for a housing commission home, and it was there I first heard the music that was to shape so much of my life. I often think this was when my life really started.

We didn't have a lot when we were at the caravan park, but one day Dad came home with an odd-looking thing that turned out to be a gramophone—a record player. He brought a round, flat, plastic thing out. I asked, 'What's that?' and he said, 'It's a record, son.'

He put the scratchy 78 on the turntable and carefully placed the needle onto its surface. I was mesmerised by all of this but then, as the sound began to come out of that record, my fascination turned to awe. The sound was Mario Lanza singing 'Serenade' from the musical *The Student Prince*. The effect was sudden, totally unexpected and, above all, riveting. During those few moments I know I didn't move, I couldn't move. I was transfixed with a joy I had never felt in my whole life. That fantastic voice and that magnificent song were so magical, so wonderful and, yes, so spiritual that I wanted to clench my fists and cry out as though I had discovered something startling and new, and yet I knew I couldn't because any movement, any sound would break the spell.

It embraced me like velvet, stilling everything about me except my heart, which was beating so fast I half wondered whether it was going to burst while the other half of me wanted it to beat even faster.

When the song came to an end I asked Dad to put it on again. And again. And again, until gradually the excitement inside me turned to something else. As the voice and the song continued to wash over me I found myself becoming immersed in it until my whole body felt as though I was singing with him. And then it was as if I was alone and that voice coming out of that recording was mine, it was actually me performing, singing on that record.

That experience was to start my life on the course it has taken. I have never lost the passion I felt that day. It is still inside me, as raw and intense as it was when I listened as an eight-year-old to a voice that transformed the person I was.

I think that from that time on a softness came into my life, a kind of comfort that, like cotton wool, was to protect me from the bad experiences and memories I carried deep within me. In hindsight I can see that I clung to the beauty and the feelings it evoked inside me as a drowning man would cling to a lifebuoy.

As I have said, a lot of my memories of early childhood are disjointed, and some I think I have tried to block out altogether, but from the time music—and that music in particular—was introduced to me, I have had a gentle place to escape to, a place where I feel happy and safe.

## CHAPTER 2

## DARWIN IN THE LATE 1960S

was still a bit of a frontier town, a melting pot of different cultures and people. I was a skinny kid with bright red curls and had become a bit of a sook, a real little mummy's boy. I might as well have had 'Bully Me' tattooed on my forehead.

I really can't say that I have any happy memories of my school days. I was an easy mark and found it safer to play with the girls than to try to fit in with the boys. I could run fast, but when you're stuck in a playground that doesn't really help much.

I did learn one quite profound lesson that has stayed with me my whole life. I was in the classroom and said something that was quite cheeky to the teacher. Whether it was intentional or not I don't remember, but I do know the rest of the class thought it was hilarious. Suddenly I felt that I had found a way to fit in, to belong—and, like most kids, I pushed it too far.

I was sent to the principal's office where I had to bend

over for the strap. The pain and humiliation was bad enough, but what made it worse was the fact that I had been pretending to be someone I wasn't. So I decided that if I was going to be belted, it might as well be for being who I was, a sooky mummy's boy, and I promptly gave up any idea of becoming a class clown.

In those days, the playgrounds were split into separate areas for boys and girls. I usually spent my lunchtimes on the border between them, and it was here one day that a gang of kids came up and wanted my lunch. I was just about to hand over my sandwich when—whack! The ringleader was punched right on the nose. It was Mandy, my little sister, sticking up for me. I never lost my lunch again. I also never lost my reputation as a mummy's boy.

Perhaps the most enduring memory I have of my childhood is of the closeness and love within our family. We might not have had much but we all looked out for each other, and Mum and Dad were the most loving parents anyone could ask for. They were strict—well, with eight kids they had to be—but never harsh or cruel. We may have moved a lot and not had much in the way of possessions, but one thing we were always secure about was the love and strength of the family.

Of course there were problems, but it is a credit to Mum and Dad that we were never drawn into any arguments they might have had. Looking back it is obvious there were issues that could well have broken up other families but, as kids, we were left blissfully unaware that anything might be wrong.

In the early days, too, I think they must have been quite homesick. Australia is so different to England; even Christmas is at the wrong time of year. There were the beautiful golden beaches and the great weather that they were probably promised in England, but it was also stinking hot with loads of flies. I think Dad in particular found it hard, because he had left all his relatives behind, whereas at least Mum had her parents and sister here.

Some of my happiest memories of those days are of spending time at my Nan's unit in Rapid Creek, a suburb of Darwin, listening to her Diana Ross records and chewing on Oddfellows mints while she taught me how to tell the time.

Nan had a huge tree growing in her backyard and right at the top was the strangest object I had ever seen. Nan told me to climb up and pick it, so I shinned up the tree and brought down this big, nutty, pale green thing. Nan broke it open and held it out for me to eat. I swear it was the sweetest, most delicious taste. It was a *real* custard apple, nothing like the ones you get in the supermarkets down south.

At Nan's place I would listen enraptured as my grandfather brought to life the music that had become so important to me. He was actually my mum's stepfather, so there was no biological connection, but I couldn't have asked for a better granddad. George Russell was his name. He was a huge man who towered over Nan and he had a very powerful tenor voice. I have no idea what drew him to sing opera, but he would sing to me from *I Pagliacci* while we were waiting for Nan's oxtail soup to cook. It's a beautiful aria, 'Vesti La Guiba', about a tragic clown putting on his face for an audience while his heart is breaking. The poignancy of the words and the memory of my grandfather give this aria a special meaning, and even today I find it difficult to sing without getting emotional.

Darwin was a fairly stable time in my life. We eventually moved to a commission house, which was lovely and new, and Dad had a good job as a foreman in a factory. I suppose that for a time we were reasonably well off. Dad would make things in the garage—trailers and bikes—and one Christmas morning I woke early to find that I had my first big bike. The excitement of riding it on that early Christmas morning is a clear memory; everything was so blue it was as though a blue filter had been put over the sky.

I was in the older group of kids in our family. Mum and Dad were busy working and looking after toddlers and babies, so Paul, Mandy and I were pretty much left to our own devices. And back in the sixties kids generally had a lot more freedom than they do today. We weren't confined by fences and backyards and were constantly having what we thought were fabulous adventures. In hindsight, and as a parent, I now recall many of them with absolute horror. There were so many times that I could have died, I really don't know how I'm still here. A lot of the stuff was very innocent and harmless, but sometimes we pushed our luck as far as we could.

New suburbs were being developed all around Darwin when we lived there. This was before Cyclone Tracy, which destroyed most of Darwin on Christmas Eve in 1974, and I remember a lot of the houses seemed to be built predominantly of sandstone. Dad had bought an old trolley and we would go around the building sites and collect the empty soft-drink bottles that the workers had thrown away. We would take these to the local milkbar and trade them for ginger strips and salty plums. The saltiness was more appealing than lollies in such a hot and humid climate.

Paul and I would often go off on bushwalks. We would traipse along for miles into the scrub and bush outside the city, always looking for adventure. One day we seemed to be in the middle of nowhere, alone in the bush with just the sounds of nature around us. Then we heard a low murmur and realised that we weren't the only ones out there. It offered us the perfect opportunity to become mini-commandos, creeping stealthily through the bush to discover an enemy camp.

Of course we might as well have been riding elephants. We rounded a track and came to a clearing where a group of tribal Aborigines were sitting in a circle. Any commando bravery we had left us as we stared at their shiny black skin and bright white teeth. They must have seen the look of fear on our faces, as they smiled and gestured for us to join them and share their food.

I don't remember how many times we visited them, but I do know that they were very gentle, generous people, with a wicked sense of humour. One time as we were sitting with them, Paul asked what we were eating. One of the older men chuckled as he drew a picture of a snake in the sand. Our reaction to this news made them all laugh. For us it was a disgusting delight. We went back after that and had possum, wallaby, goanna—you name it, we ate it.

Armed with the belief every child has, that they are indestructible, we took awful risks that seemed perfectly safe at the time. We had found a rock pool outside town, and it soon became our favourite swimming hole. We would climb to an overhanging rock and divebomb into the water. One of Paul's friends came with us once and the water was very low, it must have been in the dry season. He climbed up the rock and jumped in, and suddenly the water seemed to turn red. I stood on the side waiting for him to resurface, but he didn't. Paul was a very strong swimmer and dived down to find him. He came back to the surface, took a huge breath and dived down again, emerging with his friend in his arms.

It turned out his mate had got his leg caught on a submerged tin drum rusting away on the bottom. Paul has always been incredibly strong and I trotted beside him as he literally carried the poor kid all the way back to town in the heat. Rather than curb our enthusiasm for adventure, incidents like these reinforced our sense of indestructibility. We didn't think it was dangerous because things always worked out in the end.

The beaches in Darwin are really unusual. At low tide they look as if there is miles of sand, but then the tide comes in so fast it seems to chase you. You can see from the colour of the water where the drop-off was, where the shallow water ended; you would be looking out onto lovely, light blue water and then suddenly it was black. If there was no water it would be like standing on the top of a cliff.

One day we went right out into the water and a man said to us, 'Don't go and swim in the dark parts because there's a very strong undercurrent and it goes down for hundreds of feet.' Of course, that meant that we had to test it out.

As we swam further out, I could feel the water pulling at my legs but for some reason I didn't get frightened. I took a deep breath as the current pulled me down, further and further. When I opened my eyes I saw a huge underwater cliff-face right in front of me. For some reason I stayed calm, and then the current released me and I shot to the surface, into the brilliant sunshine. That was just one of the times I should have been killed.

Paul and I had a typical brothers' relationship. Physically he was quite different to me, very good looking with dark hair and lovely olive skin that didn't burn or freckle like mine. I would never have taken the chances we did if I were alone, but Paul had enough strength and confidence for the both of us.

Paul had decided early on that my role in life was to amuse him. He was one of the most antagonistic kids I've ever met in my life. Perhaps it was his way of toughening me up. My heart would sink when I heard the words, 'Do you want to muck around?' Then it would start: slap slap, poke poke, all the time goading me with, 'Do you want to muck around? Do you?'

I always swore to myself that was it, I would never go anywhere with him again. But I always did. He would lull me into a false sense of security. Perhaps I felt pleased that my older brother wanted to include me, so whenever he asked me to join him on a bushwalk, all my past resolve would disappear and I would trot along beside him like an obedient puppy. Then, in the middle of nowhere, I would hear the dreaded words, 'Do you want to muck around?'

Once, I can't really remember how old I was, Paul and I were at the local tip looking for treasure when we came across an old fridge. I suppose the temptation was just too great, for Paul decided to lock me in it. I think he must have forgotten about me and I have no idea of how long I stayed in there, but I wasn't missed at home until tea time when Dad asked where I was. 'Oh yeah', said Paul, 'he's in the fridge.'

I've never like confined spaces since then, which again was too great a temptation for my big brother. One of his favourite ways to torment me over the years was to wrap me from head to foot in a blanket and sit on me so I couldn't move.

I couldn't outrun Paul when I was little, and I've lost count of the times I put myself at his mercy. Looking back, I often wonder whether he was trying to make me face my fears and so overcome them. Although Paul and I never discussed the abduction he must have been affected by it, too. Perhaps his role as older brother and protector had been challenged by what had happened to me and Mandy.

In spite of all the teasing, Paul was, and still is, one of the most generous people I've ever known. Our gypsy lifestyle meant that being the new kid at school was a common experience for us. We never really got to form friendships like most kids do, so we developed traditions of mateship within the family.

Anyone who's ever gone to a new school will know that awful feeling of having a classroom full of kids looking at you, checking you out. Standing in front of those staring eyes, you know they are counting every freckle, noticing every blemish, taking you in as they concoct painful nicknames. And as you blush you know that you are revealing your soul, your fear is laid bare to their hungry eyes. There is no escape, they've got you, you are theirs to torment or befriend, depending on their appraisal. I've lost count of the number of new schools we went to but I never got used to that 'new kid' feeling.

It's probably quite ironic that today I actually put myself on show; it is on stage that I can truly be me and reveal the passion inside. Perhaps the difference is that I choose to be on stage, it is me who is in control. Maybe the memory of the classroom lingers, but as always in my life it is the singing that gives me strength.

One school in particular stands out because of the initiation ceremony held by the boys. Paul and I were bailed up on the first day and told that we had a choice of three initiations. The first was to stand behind a door and not move as the gang of boys ran at the door full pelt, hammering the person on the other side. The second was to have your head held down the toilet while they took it in turns to pee on you. The third was to be stripped naked, taken to the girls' playground, turned upside-down and, with a kid holding each leg, get walloped with an iron bar between the legs.

The fear I felt as I looked at this junior gang of sadists must have been like that felt by a man facing the gallows. Of course, dobbing wasn't an option and anyway the boys told me that if I ever told a soul then they would get me later and I would have to endure all three initiations, instead of just one.

I didn't have to lie to my parents about how ill I felt, but try as I might, I couldn't get out of going to school the next day. To say my legs were trembling would be an understatement. My whole body felt like jelly as I waited for the torture to begin. Paul was in the year ahead of me so he went first. He had already decided that the door was the least of the three evils. He braced himself behind the door as the little thugs charged at him one by one, and emerged to ask them if that was the best they could do. Then he looked over at me, his skinny little brother who had turned to a gibbering mess. I'll never forget what he said next as he nodded in my direction. 'I'll do his for him.'

I stared at my brother, only a kid himself, and knew at that moment that he was the strongest, bravest person I'd ever met.

But the gang had their tradition and having a substitute wasn't on. I was unable to even speak by this stage so they decided for me. It was to be the playground strip and bash. As they marched me towards the girls' play area I began to sob uncontrollably, taking in huge gasps of air as I tried to beg for mercy. The mob mentality had taken over, and I was surrounded by kids who wanted to see pain and humiliation.

Just when it seemed that my fate was sealed, a huge hand reached over and landed on the head of the ringleader. It was Big John, a kid who was probably about fifteen but had been kept back in primary school because he was 'slow'. He was huge, with the body of a man but the brain of a child.

I was to learn later that John loved watching this one particular western show on TV. Now was his chance to play the role of the hero. He looked at my tormentor and, in the cowboy drawl he had heard so often, said, 'You're acting mighty hasty, son. Touch him, and you'll have to deal with me.' That was it. The crowd dispersed, and Big John had a new friend for the rest of the time that we were at that awful school.

I don't have a clear memory of leaving Darwin and I don't think that any of us kids really knew why we left, but one day we packed up the car and headed off again. Any confusion we felt about the move had become a normal part of our childhood—we'd learned early on in life not to get too settled or comfortable, as we would inevitably be on the move again.

There were six of us kids by the time we left. One of Dad's mates from the factory wanted to head to the east coast, so he came with us too. We were very cramped, lying in the back of the station wagon fighting like bloody cats and dogs.

Whenever we were on the road Paul would be in great form. He would burp and blow in my face, he'd poke and prod, always starting with those dreaded words, 'You want to muck around?' Dad's mate—we called him Uncle Ted— offered a bit of a diversion for us on this trip. He spoke very slowly, pausing for about three seconds after each word, and we thought this was hilarious. We gave him merry hell, just to hear him say, 'You . . . kids . . . cut . . . it . . . out.' We were very easily amused in those days.

Poor Uncle Ted, he didn't have much chance with us around. I suppose we were bored and perhaps part of me was glad that Paul had someone else to amuse him. Where Uncle Ted was concerned, I became a very willing apprentice to my older brother. We could be really sadistic little buggers, like the time when he was asleep in his chair with his cigarette still burning. He used to smoke rollies, and we had to gently remove his smoke without waking him. His feet were bare, and we placed the burning cigarette between his toes, facing down so that it would burn up. Then we waited, mentally counting down to his explosion.

'Aah! Ya . . . bloody . . . mongrels!' Ted was quite big and lumbering, and his voice was a bellow like a bull about to charge. We loved it when he'd chase us. We knew he would never catch us, but we still loved the thrill of being chased.

We were quite ingenious another time. Ted loved Sao biscuits covered in Vegemite. Paul got hold of some of Mum's laxative pills and hid them in the bubbles of the biscuits, then we smothered butter and Vegemite over the top. I did feel a bit guilty. Ted was so thrilled that we had made his favourite snack, and he ate the whole lot. We had to wait a bit longer for the explosion this time. It was about four o'clock in the morning, on Ted's sixth trip to the toilet, when we heard him mutter through the door, 'Ya . . . bloody . . . mongrels.'

From Darwin we travelled to Townsville, stopping along the way at various campsites and caravan parks. We must have stayed at Townsville for a while because I have a memory of catching the ferry across to Magnetic Island, which was quite exciting. To a kid it was like going overseas.

We moved on through lots of towns, some we stayed at for a few days, others for longer, but my recall of those times is a little hazy. Even Mum and Dad have forgotten all the places we went to. Dad would pick up work wherever we went. He could do just about anything, I've seen him pull car engines apart and put them back together without anyone showing him how. Even today he builds the most beautiful furniture in his garage at home. People come from miles around to buy the things he makes, all through word of mouth.

Dad and I were very close and I have many memories of just him and me doing things together like fishing and hunting. Whether the other kids were with us I don't really know, but it says a lot about our relationship that I remember those times as belonging to us.

We lived for a time at a place outside Taree in New

South Wales called Latimore's Farm. It was a beautiful old Victorian-style farmhouse on top of a big hill surrounded by miles and miles of land. Sometimes it seemed that in some of the places we stayed, time lasted forever, because we loved living in a real house so much. We probably weren't at the farm for any more than two or three months but it seems like longer as I look back.

My Dad had been trained as a marksman in the army and when we were on the farm he would take me hunting. He also knew exactly how to snare rabbits. He'd make these little traps out of wire and place them around the burrows before nightfall. The rabbits would run out of their burrows into the snares and be killed instantly. In the morning we'd go down and there would be dead rabbits everywhere.

Dad didn't like killing things, and he certainly didn't hunt for fun, but when you've got no money and hungry children, you do these things. Sometimes I would say to him, 'Dad, let's get some more.' He'd always tell me, 'Son, we've got enough to eat. Don't kill anything unless you're going to eat it.'

That farm holds some terrific memories. My sister, Mandy, and I walked for miles on the farm. Physically Mandy was a lot like me, a skinny little red-head. Our relationship was very special and gentle. We spent a lot of time together and although we never spoke about what had happened to us, I think this was our way of reconnecting and creating happy times for ourselves. We'd had enough danger to last forever. We used to sing together a lot, practising songs from musicals like *The Sound of Music* and *My Fair Lady*.

On one of our walks we came across what must have been an old homesite because there was a big concrete slab on the ground and a little shed. It was here that we found eight trees full of mandarins. It was like Aladdin's cave, this golden fruit waiting to be picked. For some reason we decided to pick all of them—it seemed like thousands. We loaded up the old shed with mandarins and gorged ourselves, then we took a load back to the house. We wouldn't tell anyone where we had found them, it was our secret.

We were at the mandarin trees one day when we decided to hike to the top of a huge hill, where it seemed as though the horizon stopped and the land ended. When we got to the top, it was like something out of *Tom Sawyer*. We were standing looking down at this huge river that looked as big as the Mississippi. The side of the hill leading to the river, was almost a cliff, and we sat up there and felt as if we were flying. Just sitting high on the hill and eating our mandarins gave us the most beautiful feeling of freedom. It was like sitting on top of the world.

Times like that were really important to us, I suppose because we were restricted so much, being stuck in the car.

Mixed with the happy times were times when we knew that we weren't like other kids. A car was no substitute for a real home and we had to learn to adapt and compensate, as all kids do. So for us Christmas was always a magic time, especially when we were living in a house. When we woke up on Christmas mornings, our beds would be covered in chocolates and lollies and toys and things. We would get up and the lounge-room would be full and the Christmas tree would be laden with presents. Mum and Dad would save and do whatever they could to give us the best Christmas; we really had it laid on. This was in huge contradiction to the rest of the year, when at times we had next to nothing.

Two or three months later all our presents would have to be sold or given away because we would be in the car again; we never got to keep anything. This reinforced for us that nothing else was permanent, the only thing that was stable and solid was the family. The only toy I ever kept was a teddy bear Mum made me from scraps of old material. I called him Sinbad, and I loved him. He was my friend. I can remember saying to Mum, 'Can I keep this?' and I was so happy when she told me I could. I carried that bloody thing around with me for most of my young life.

The gramophone and the records was another thing we always kept; music remained a constant in my life. Singing seemed to be a part of it, whether it was the big booming voice of my granddad or the lovely tenor sound of my father as he peeled potatoes at the sink. As I've said, that first song, 'Serenade', stayed with me. I listened over and over to that record, committing the notes, the tone, the feel of that song to memory. I would practise and practise with my little boy's screech in the shower, singing until my throat hurt.

Who knows why the effect was so powerful, but a few years after I first heard the song, Dad bought the LP that 'Serenade' was on and I had the same intense experience when I looked at the album cover as when I first heard the song. It sounds weird, even to me, but as I looked at Mario Lanza's face, I found myself looking into my own eyes. I actually started crying; the likeness in our eyes was uncanny. I learned later that Mario Lanza died sixteen days before I was born, so we were never on the earth at the same time. As a child I often wondered whether part of his spirit had been hovering, waiting for me to be born.

One thing I do know is that part of Lanza has stayed with me since that first time. His influence, his voice, gave me the courage to be who I was. Through all the different schools, the constant travelling and the uncertainty, I would come back to music for strength and safety. At times when it seemed there was nothing to sing about, singing became everything.

BEHIND MY VOICE

CHAPTER 3

## DAD TOLD ME HE COUNTED 79 MOVES

over the years. He reckons he stopped adding up the distance we travelled after we clocked up more than a million miles.

We thought nothing of it as kids and the experiences we had can't be found in a classroom or school books. We swam in Katherine Gorge, watched the sun come up at Uluru, got caught in dust storms in deserts and became stranded by flood waters in Dubbo as hailstones as big as cricket balls rained down on the car while we huddled inside, scared and excited all at the same time. There were times when we were quite well off, living in a house with a swimming pool and all the mod cons, and other times when we have been literally destitute.

There was the time we left Townsville and picked up a hitchhiker. I have no idea where he sat but he travelled with us all the way to Brisbane. The car was brand new and, seeing that it was packed with all the gear we could carry, it must have been a cramped journey. When we arrived in Brisbane, we all piled out of the car and the guy offered to find a parking spot while Mum and Dad took us with them and sorted out where we were all going to stay. We never saw the hitchhiker, the car or any of our stuff again.

We had absolutely nothing but the clothes we were standing in. I don't know what would have happened to us if it wasn't for the Salvation Army. They found us somewhere to stay, gave us clothes and some money and helped Dad get on his feet again. The help they gave seemed limitless and I can't speak highly enough of the work they do. 'Thank God for the Salvos' is far more than a catchy slogan for me.

While we were staying at the Salvation Army hostel, another thing happened that has stayed with me my whole life. Mum was heavily pregnant at the time and she was in the communal laundry, where there were about eight machines, all in use by one woman. I don't know what was said but it ended up in a fight between Mum and this woman, who kicked her in the stomach. I stood petrified at the sight of all the blood, but I think the worst thing was watching Dad cry as he cradled Mum in his arms while she gave birth on the floor of that filthy laundry. The baby was stillborn, one of three such tragedies Mum had to live through as time went by.

Then there was the old car we called the, 'I think I can car'. It was after we had left Brisbane and we were travelling through the Blue Mountains in New South Wales with their massive straight-up-and-down hills. The car was okay so long as Dad could get up enough speed going downhill to get a good run up the next. He would race down, like the big dipper, and we always just made it over the top and down the other side. But then we got stuck behind a truck that was just putt-putting along. Dad knew there was no way he would make it up the next hill because the car didn't have enough power to overtake the truck.

And, sure enough, the car conked out halfway up the hill before slowly starting to roll back the way we had come. I'm not sure what happened next but we spun out of control and the back half of the car ended up over the edge of a cliff at the side of the road.

We had all started screaming, convinced we were about to plummet to our deaths, when Dad took charge. He has always been a very calm, stoic sort of bloke, a man of few words. So when he speaks people generally listen. Dad sat very calmly behind the wheel and, instead of shouting and bellowing out orders, he simply asked each of us kids, quietly and one by one, to climb from the back of the car to the front. Other than the softness of his voice there was a deathly silence inside the car, but from outside came an ominous creaking as our bodies moved and gradually shifted the weight from the back to the front. When he was sure the car was balanced right, Dad slowly opened the door and climbed out to go for help.

We were in the middle of nowhere. I don't know how long we waited, squashed together in the front of the car, but it seemed like an eternity before Dad arrived back with the NRMA, who pulled the car to safety.

I must have been about ten or eleven when we moved to the Sydney suburb of Dee Why. I have very happy memories of our time there, especially the days we spent as kids on the

Manly Pier, which wasn't far away. At the end of the pier there was a fairground with a ferris wheel and other rides. There was a lovely lady who sold fairy floss and who was always dressed in pink. I would buy her a cup of Bonox and she would pay me with the sugar that came from the bottom of the fairy floss machine.

Paul and I would hitchhike to the pier and fish for yellow-tail which we sold to an old lady who bought them to feed her cats. Paul would often dive off the pier for money the tourists would throw in for him. We would also bludge for money, telling people that we had lost our bus fare and needed to get home. This backfired one time when a kind man put us on the bus and paid our fare. I don't know why, but we didn't think to get off at the next stop and we ended up going all the way home. We would use the money we got to go on the rides or catch a ferry around the harbour.

I loved this one particular ferry called the *South Steyne*. It was bigger than the others and to us it was like being on a proper ship. Going past the heads was always a bit scary as it could be rough sometimes. But once past, the water became calm again. There was one occasion when we had just reached the heads and the engines cut out; the sea was so rough that when I looked over the side to what I thought was the sky I found myself staring at a huge wall of water. The skipper kept his head and showed what a good seaman he was, letting the boat take each wave so that we ran uphill from one side of a wave and down the other until finally the engines restarted.

For some reason I was really drawn to the ferries; I can remember thinking that when I grew up I wanted to buy a boat just like the *South Steyne*. One really happy memory I have of that ferry is when I met a lovely couple. At the time I thought of them as elderly, but they were probably only in their thirties. I was always singing and they heard me and we got chatting. With all the confidence of a ten-year-old I told them that I was going to be a famous singer one day. Whether they were just humouring me or not I don't know, but the woman took a pen and piece of paper from her bag. She gave me a big smile as she said, 'We'll write your name down now so that we don't forget it.' I sometimes wonder if those people are still out there today.

There was a time, though, when a ferry and a wall of water weren't so friendly. Paul and I were, as usual, fishing from under the Manly Pier, and we'd clambered along the web of beams that made up its supports so that we could get to the end of the pier where the deep water was. All of a sudden I heard a noise. I looked up and there was a wall of water coming towards us. I screamed out to Paul as we realised that it was the wash created by the ferry coming alongside. We took off so fast we didn't bother to look behind us as we raced along the beams, hearing the roar of the wave as it came tearing along under the pier. We lost our rods and everything but managed to make it to dry land. It was only then that we looked behind and saw the wave crash against the jetty wall.

Nothing seemed to worry Paul. He tackled everything as though it was a dare or some kind of adventure and the surf beach was nothing more than a challenge. On rough days, especially after a storm, you could look out over the black, deep water and see where sandbanks had formed. I lost count of the times Paul was dragged out of the water by boats as he swam out to the sandbanks, just a little black dot bobbing in the waves. But he was a very strong swimmer and he soon became a junior lifesaver.

Paul decided to teach me how to body surf. It was a particularly rough day and the waves seemed to be enormous. Where I saw danger Paul saw fun. I was scared stiff as we stood there in the water waiting for the waves. Then we saw the huge swell approaching. Paul told me to swim as fast as I could to catch it and ride it in. Then it was on us. I just didn't have enough strength and I remember Paul yelling out to me to hold my breath as he shot off on top of the wave towards the shore. When I eventually surfaced I found I was behind the wave, and I couldn't work out why I was standing on the sand with the beach itself such a long way away.

Then I realised why—it was a double wave. The second wave was coming. Instinct must have kicked in because I managed to take a huge breath just before it hit me, tossing me around like dirty clothes in a washing machine. I was not a strong swimmer but I used all the strength I could find to push my body towards what I was convinced was the surface. But then I banged into sand. I had become so disorientated I'd swum downwards. So I planted my feet on the sand and pushed as hard as I could. The waves were on my side this time because the next thing I knew, I was lying on the beach with Paul standing over me.

It was around this time that Paul and I got mixed up with a group of boys who had found an empty two-storey house that they used as a clubhouse. It was a funny kind of place with the upper and lower rooms exactly the same. It was as if the walls and doorways extended right to the ground, with the upper floor being added later. Still, it was a great place to meet because, among other things, it meant we were part of a gang. I don't know about Paul but I was petrified of those boys. We both did as we were told, out of fear or a need to fit in, or perhaps both.

In those days the milkman would deliver bottles to people's doors and money would be left out for him the night before. And of course it was all too easy. Dee Why was made up of loads of blocks of flats without much security and so all the gang had to do was go around and take the money from under the empty milk bottles. I knew what we were doing was wrong but at the same time it was wonderful to have all that money. It was all in coins so we pinched some of Dad's socks to keep it together.

We actually made the local news—'Milkos Strike Again'—and we thought we were really clever. That is, until we came home one day and Dad's face told us he had found our hoard. He would have, naturally, but we'd been too stupid and cocky to realise it. Still, he knocked all the arrogance out of us by making us go round to all the houses and return the money we'd stolen.

Not long after that little episode we found ourselves on the road again, this time staying for a while at Dubbo, where we lived in an eight-man tent and picked asparagus. It was at Dubbo that the most violent hailstorm I've ever seen swept the tent away and almost took us with it. The whole incident was eerie. I remember us standing in a paddock on a beautiful sunny day, watching as the storm approached. Then we saw that the sun was glistening on a wall of white hailstones. It was just a shimmering mass in the distance at first but then, within seconds, this horrendous wall of white stones hit us. All we could do was stand helpless as it swept across our campsite, pelting and ruining our tent and soaking everything we owned.

It was on this trip that we stayed at another farmhouse for a while, and I have happy memories of the time Mandy and I spent with a dear old man on one of the neighbouring farms. His name was Edgar and he was probably well into his nineties when we knew him. We spent many hours listening to tales of his life as a rouseabout, bringing herds of wild horses in from the mountains and travelling along stock routes around the country.

His mind was probably going a bit and he spoke with a speech impediment, so that as he was telling a story he would intersperse what he was saying with the phrase 'peek, peek and pook'. Poor Edgar had no idea he was doing it and sometimes Mandy and I would sit there, entranced by the stories while at the same time trying so hard not to laugh.

With the natural curiosity of children, we took the time to listen to the people we met. As we were rarely in a classroom for any length of time, we used experiences like this as a chance to learn. Edgar taught me how to make butter. He had a house cow called Daisy and we would milk her and churn the milk for the butter which I would take home to Mum and Dad.

After the farm we made our way down to Ardmona, a huge fruit-picking area near Shepparton in country Victoria. Memories of Ardmona signal for me the end of my childhood. We were there from about 1971 to 1974, so it was there that I moved into my teens.

We stayed for a while in a caravan park at nearby Mooroopna. As was the pattern in our lives, we moved around a lot in the area, picking tomatoes and fruit before moving into an old house on one of the orchards where Dad got a job. The house was pretty dilapidated when we moved in, but Dad soon fixed it up and even added a couple of rooms out the back for Paul and me.

It seems odd, but, whenever we stayed in one place for longer than a few weeks, we would put down roots, settle for a while and even plan or build, almost like normal families. One time Dad even built me a coop for homing pigeons. I loved those birds but in my eagerness to set them free released them too early and they joined another flock and never came home. As a kid I thought that maybe it wasn't my fault. Perhaps, like us kids, they knew not to get too comfortable as we would soon be on the move again.

Mooroopna High was the last school I ever attended. The school consisted mainly of portables, although there was an old building that was part of the original school. It sat in a flat, nondescript landscape, and the only memories I have of that place are filled with dread.

Racial tension between Aborigines and non-Aborigines was an issue around Shepparton, and the place it was most likely to surface was at school. I was used to being bullied at school and, thinking back, I suppose there was an air about me of expecting someone to do something that made me a tempting target. I was a skinny, gangly kid, so I didn't offer much to thugs in the way of a challenge and I certainly never tried to be tough or full of bravado like many boys my age. Whatever the reason, from my first day at that school I was the punching bag for the local Aboriginal gang.

The abuse was constant and became a part of my life, so much so that I would just be walking through the school-yard or down a corridor and the head of the gang, a boy named Leo, would make a beeline for me to punch me in the stomach or trip me over as I walked past. Fear became part of who I was. No matter how much I tried to avoid them, they would always find me. I don't know that they deliberately hunted me down but whenever they came across me it was always the same—a punch, a whack and me ending up on my back with them standing around laughing.

I have never understood the mentality or the emotion behind violence. To deliberately hurt another person for no reason other than your own amusement is just incomprehensible to me. I have heard theories that poverty and a poor upbringing can foster the culture of violence. But our upbringing wasn't exactly idyllic, and we were certainly exposed to violence of the most horrific type when Mandy and I were abducted. And the constant bullying I had to put up with throughout my school life never led me to think that I too should try to be a bully so that in some perverse way I might avoid it by inflicting it on others.

So it continued, day in, day out, the fists and feet of my attackers becoming as much a part of my schooling as the lessons I was meant to learn.

Then one day one of the girls told me the gang was planning to get me and give me a proper bashing after school. There was a rumour around town that they had attacked a kid on his way to the shops and he had ended up dead. So I had no doubts about what a 'proper bashing' meant. The girl helped me leave school by a back fence and I ran all the way home to tell Mum and Dad what was happening.

I know Dad spoke to the school but he obviously didn't get very far because it was decided I should leave and continue my schooling by correspondence. Education was never a high priority in our family. With so many moves it was often a hindrance, particularly as we got older and of an age when we could have been earning a wage. Also, as we moved so much, the last year of school that I actually completed was grade five, so high school was always going to be a struggle. It was with some relief that my school days came to an end.

But even though I'd left, I was still petrified of the gang because, as I was to learn in the weeks to come, they were out for revenge for having missed me when they'd wanted to get me. I lost count of the number of times they beat me up, so often that just going into Shepparton filled me with dread. They always seemed to be there, outside the coffee shop, on a street corner, near the cinema. So today, all those places that should hold happy memories of my early teens instead evoke images of beatings and humiliation.

As in most country towns the annual local show in Mooroopna was a huge social event. For the farmers, the graziers and fruit growers, it was their chance to show off their prize animals or produce and for kids it provided a taste of fun and excitement. Naturally our only interest was in the sideshows and the rides.

Dad took a load of us in one night and gave us all some spending money, so I remember it as being pretty special. I was standing at the entrance with my little sister Josie, waiting for Dad to park the car, when all the excitement bubbling around inside me evaporated. From the darkness of the trees I saw the gang approaching. I didn't have time to run. As soon as I saw Leo's face I knew that I had made his night; the show was going to be more fun than he had thought. They started laying into me, and poor little Josie ran screaming to find Dad.

By the time he got there they had gone and I was lying on the ground, bleeding and crying. Dad was not a big man and most of the time he was very gentle, but if anyone hurt a member of his family his fury would erupt. He picked me up, took me to the car and we drove slowly around the streets of the town. We found Leo. He was on his own. Dad leapt from the car and grabbed him by the throat. Leo must have seen something in his eyes because he didn't utter a word and simply let Dad give him a hiding and tell him never to come near me again.

Much later in life I studied martial arts and eventually became a black belt in karate. At the beginning my sole intention was to return to that town and beat up all the people who had made my life a living hell. But as I learned more I came to realise self-defence is not about being tough or picking fights. I have only had to use my martial arts skills once, and I think the simple act of learning it and realising what it means has not only taught me to quell my fears and given me more confidence but has also erased that 'Bully Me' sign which for years I was convinced I carried around with me.

I got my first real job fairly soon after leaving school, so that was the end of my education by correspondence. I was working for a man called Charlie, the foreman at a local orchard. Charlie was a wonderful person; he had a pink complexion with really white hair, a typical Australian-looking sort of guy.

I started work in the off-season, fixing up the fruit bins. I was only fourteen but Charlie let me drive the forklift. And

I had a ball, tearing around the orchards, until one day I got a bit cocky and backed into a brand-new car parked by the sheds. The car belonged to the owner of the orchard.

He really let me have it, which I suppose was fair enough since I'd just wrecked his car. Even so, he was one of those men who seemed to relish the chance to throw their weight around. As he was yelling at me, Charlie came into the shed and eventually calmed him down, convincing him it was an accident that could have happened to anyone. Then Charlie and his wife took me out to lunch.

A few days later the owner called me out to a paddock where he and his father were standing next to a trailer with a magnificent bull standing inside. It was a beautiful beast but as I stood there looking at it I suddenly heard a loud bang and the bull fell to the floor. The father then leapt astride the animal and took out a huge knife to slit its throat. Then they yelled at me to grab hold of it and help drag it out of the trailer. But as we were dragging it, the bull somehow managed to pull itself up. The poor thing was still alive! It was horrific, watching this animal struggle to its feet, blood pouring from its throat. Then bang, bang, bang! They shot it again, three times and, finally, down it went.

I couldn't believe what I was seeing. I ran away screaming at them, 'You can't even kill it properly!'

When Charlie came to the sheds later that day he could see I'd been crying. His pink face turned scarlet when I told him what had happened and he ran straight to the office where he confronted the owner. I can remember Charlie yelling at him, 'For God's sake, you know he's not like other kids. Why can't you leave him alone?'

I suppose every teenager goes through a stage when they think they are different from everyone else. But hearing Charlie say it confirmed for me two lessons I already knew. One was that I really *was* different from other kids and there was something about me that would rub some people up the wrong way. I wasn't completely weird, but I was happy in my own company, and people still saw me as a bit of a sook or mummy's boy.

The other lesson was that not all bullies are children.

Our collection of musical records and tapes had grown by this time. So too had my interest in singers. I had already realised I too had a bit of singing voice and Elvis and Roy Orbison in particular were two entertainers I tried to copy. I'd listen to their songs on my tape recorder in the packing sheds and decided I would become The Great Impersonator. My ability to mimic developed over the years and by the time I was an older teenager and young adult my repertoire had increased to the extent that I managed to get a lot of work on the strength of my impersonations.

But I always came back to what for me was something more meaningful. I didn't know it at the time but I came to learn that it was something they called serious music—opera.

I had no idea why, as the world of opera was so far removed from me and the life I led that it might as well have been on the other side of the moon. But something—and I didn't know what—kept pulling me back to it. All I knew was that I loved it with a passion that filled my day with dreams and kept me awake at night. Perhaps it was only natural that opera and I should become so inseparable because in many ways opera is the embodiment of music and song, of expressing life's turmoil—both tragedy and joy—through the voice. My life was certainly tumultuous, and my passion for singing was perhaps my way of dealing with things, with making sense of the life I was living.

So, in my own ungainly, uneducated and totally uninitiated way, I practised my opera in the orchards, singing what I thought were the words to the songs. As long as I had the notes and the tone of the song right, the words seemed irrelevant. (About eighteen months ago, when I first started Italian lessons, my teacher was horrified when I told her that I would sing 'Messy Doormat' instead of 'Nessun Dorma', but back then it didn't matter.) My voice would echo around the fruit trees and I soon earned the nickname 'Caruso'. Then one day I was actually asked to sing at a barbecue held by one of the big Italian families in the area.

The Italian community around Shepparton had successfully incorporated the best parts of their rich culture into the Australian way of life. Their language and traditions were part of who they were, and so it was perhaps a little odd that I, a scrawny red-haired pommy migrant, should be asked to provide the musical backdrop to one of their social occasions. None of this was relevant to me back then; I just knew that they wanted me to perform the music I loved.

I sang my heart out that day and, surprisingly, I don't think I was nervous for one moment. I was so happy that I think the excitement and adrenalin were what kept me going. There were crowds of people there and it didn't matter that I had no idea what I was singing. I just made sounds rather than actual words. I felt that I was being me. This was who I was supposed to be. The reality of my everyday life told me otherwise, but deep inside me a voice kept saying, 'This is it, one day you really will sing opera.'

I also did a lot of normal teenage stuff of course, usually tagging along after Paul. Most of the kids in the area had trail bikes that we would hoon around on. I used to ride a little Honda 125. One day I was tearing up a track, having managed to get the bike going flat out when I hit a tree head on. The bike skidded away, and I was left wrapped around the tree, with my feet pretty well touching my head. I was winded, but that was it, so I guess that's another time when my life could have ended.

One of Paul's mates went missing one night. He and a friend had been out trail-bike riding and didn't return home. The next day they found Paul's mate alive, sitting bolt upright, staring at the bushes in front of him. The poor guy had been sitting there all night, unable to move. The pillion passenger he had been carrying was staring back, eyes wide open. His body was lying about six feet away. The poor guy had gone into shock, staring at the decapitated head of his friend, still with the helmet on. My days as a budding bikie ended pretty soon after that.

Both Paul and I eventually got ourselves girlfriends. I can't speak for Paul, but my relationship with Mary-Anne was very innocent, lots of hand-holding and kissing. We actually didn't have much choice, as it seemed like every time we were together Mary-Anne's little sister Jeanette would tag along. She was only a few years younger than we were, but at that age it made all the difference. She always seemed to be with us and was incredibly annoying, as only little sisters can be.

My heart would drop when I went to meet Mary-Anne and saw this little nuisance by her side. Any wrong move on my part and we would hear the words, 'I'm telling Mum and Dad', in that awful sing-song tone little girls seem to learn at an early age. I didn't know it at the time, but the influence Jeanette was to have on my life was to be far greater than just ruining my love-life with her sister.

The adventures with Paul continued, always containing that little element of danger that made them worthwhile. Shepparton is an area that can be hit by the worst weather extremes. It was around the early 1970s when torrential rains almost swallowed the township. We had ridden into town and rested our bikes against a shop wall—it wasn't long before they were completely submerged. I am one of the few people who can say that they have swum through the streets of Shepparton.

It became apparent while we were at Ardmona that Mum and Dad were having some problems. Whether it was that I was older and took more notice or whether the problems had only just surfaced, I don't really know. A lot of stuff was kept from us; it was their business and should remain that way. But I know now that a lot of the issues they faced led to our life on the road, the constant travelling and moving.

Poor Mum sometimes had a problem with alcohol in the early years and things got pretty bad at one stage. I think for Mum's whole life she has been searching for something that has eluded her. New places, new babies, nothing seemed to fill the void she felt inside, so at times she looked for happiness in the bottom of a bottle. Eventually, she was admitted to a rehabilitation hospital, and the whole family went back to Sydney to stay with my grandparents who had moved to Manly.

It was a very sad time without Mum. Dad was very quiet and lonely. Paul and I revisited the old haunts, the pier and beaches, and for a while there Paul went a bit off the rails and became a bit of a street kid. Dad did the best he could, but he was like half a person, and I remember those days as being very painful and difficult for all of us. It was as if the one thing we could count on, the family, was crumbling around us and we could only stand and watch.

I don't think I've ever met anyone who loves their partner as much as Dad loves Mum. Sometimes things must have been pretty bad between them, but the thought that the family would break up, that we wouldn't see it through together was never an option. Things must have been tough for Mum too, dragging eight kids around the country, sometimes not even having a proper roof over our heads. But we never doubted her love for us.

When Mum got out of hospital we went back to Ardmona, but things weren't the same. Sadness and uncertainty settled over us like a dark cloud, and it was hard to find joy in anything. We were going through the motions, but the challenges our family faced seemed insurmountable. Mum and Dad were caught up in their own issues, and it must have been hard for them to consider the feelings of all the kids as well. There was no overt nastiness, but kids are perceptive, and I learned the meaning of the term 'to cut the air with a knife'.

I don't know what would have happened had we stayed there, living our half-life. Then one day Dad won nine hundred dollars at the races, which was a lot of money in our book. He decided it was time to make a fresh start, and so the whole family moved to the other side of the country, to Perth.

## CHAPTER 4

## THE REST OF THE FAMILY PILED INTO THE CAR

and Dad left me with a bus ticket so I could travel across and
join them in Perth. I had to finish up my work with Charlie,
so it was about a week after they left that I headed west
across the Nullarbor.

The trip was long and gave me a lot of time to think
about things, the life I was leaving and the new life I was
going to. I remember it as exciting and one of the first times
I felt independent or grown up. (I was about fifteen by
then). I wasn't cramped in a car with the rest of the family;
I was on my own and in a coach, travelling hundreds of
miles across this vast country. I'd rarely been alone in my life,
yet I'd often felt lonely. Although there were other passengers on the bus, I was alone, and I became aware of the
peace that can bring.

One of the stops was at Port Augusta. As I got off I
noticed a group of Aboriginal men sitting and watching the
passengers as they stretched their legs. I immediately thought

of Leo and his gang and my heart was thumping as I passed them to go into the shop. Then one of the men caught my eye and smiled as he said, 'G'day mate. How's it going?'

It was a genuine smile and a genuine greeting from one stranger to another. Nothing more. Nothing hidden behind those eyes. I think I realised then that I had become like all those people over the years who had tormented and bullied me. I had started to judge and, worse, to suspect people simply by their appearance. And it dawned on me then that Leo's behaviour had nothing to do with his colour; he was a bully and a thug who just happened to be Aboriginal. So from that time on I have taken people as they are.

Perth was a bright, sunny city and looked to be just the right place for a new start. It seemed as if we had put thousands of miles between us and our past, and I remember how wonderful it felt to have the family back together in such a fresh place. Our house was in a suburb called Wanneroo and to us it was real luxury—we even had a swimming pool.

Paul and I got jobs pretty quickly working at a poultry farm. It was a huge complex, like a suburban shopping centre. They did everything there—hatched the chicks, grew them, processed the meat birds for the supermarkets and grew the hens for their eggs. They even made the feed for the chickens. Paul worked in the hatchery and I was in the feed section.

They employed their own chemist to mix the vitamins that went into the feed. He was a great bloke who had been a body builder in his younger days, and had actually won the Mr Australia Body Building title once. I'd spend my whole lunchtimes with him and he'd often help me to work on my body, using the big rubber bands the factory had for sealing the feed bins so that he could work on specific muscles in my arms and back. He taught me the difference between muscle bulk and muscle strength and that the bigger and bulkier you are, the slower you are. I worked on strength rather than bulk, as speed and the ability to run away were things I was not willing to let go.

The feed travelled along a huge conveyor belt that wound its way around the factory with different things being added through openings, or gates, along the way. The conveyor was powered by a huge auger, like a massive corkscrew, that pushed the belt along. I was petrified of the machines as to me they looked so big that if you fell in you would be pulped and there'd be nothing left of you but chicken feed—and there was no such thing as work safety back then.

One day I was walking from the main building towards the lunch room when the foreman called me over and told me to climb up to the top level where the auger had jammed. I couldn't believe what I was hearing. The huge belt snaked up almost to the roof of the factory, at least a hundred feet above us. I looked at the foreman to see if he was joking, but he just carried on with the instructions.

'One of the gates is jammed with food, so you'll have to stick your hand in and clean it out,' he said. He must have seen my absolute terror at what he was saying because, almost as an afterthought, he added, 'Don't worry. We'll turn the machinery off.'

I was in a fear-driven daze as I made my way up the ladder. I don't know how I managed to put one foot in front of the other along the top of the conveyor belt, but somehow I made my way to the gate. The edge of the machine came up to my chest, so I had to lean down into the opening to clear away the feed that was blocking it. I stood for what seemed ages, staring at the huge metal corkscrew, convinced it would suck me into the machine and that I'd end up as pulp, never to be seen again.

Turning back wasn't an option, so I decided to test how far I could reach into the machine. My plan was to whip my hand in and out in about one second. If I'd been staring at the jaws of a crocodile I think I'd have felt safer. I took a deep breath and shoved my left arm down as far as it would go, past the twisted metal and on to the blocked gate.

That's when I heard the noise, a low hum, then a clunk, then a crunch. Someone had started the machine! The timing was to the millisecond. I suppose that's how it is with most accidents, a series of coincidences that culminate in tragedy. My arm couldn't have been in there for more than the blink of an eye, but that's when the machine started. And just as I was pulling my arm out the metal dug into my flesh and I could feel it dislocating and crunching the bones. There I was, perched thirty metres in the air, trapped with my arm caught in that horrifying machine and unable to do a thing about it.

I don't remember feeling any real pain, more of a scorching sensation like you got when someone twisted your skin in what we called the Chinese burn. But there was that horrifying sense of absolute nausea at the thought of having to spend the rest of my life with only one arm. The fear of being dragged in or, at the very least, losing a limb overwhelmed me and I found myself screaming at the top of my lungs, hoping that someone down below would hear me. A man who looked about five centimetres tall from where I was looked up, then raised his arms above his head as he ran to the machine room. Then came the low droning buzz of the whole factory being shut down and I guessed someone had pulled some kind of emergency lever.

I was convinced my arm had been severed and, because I didn't want to see the stump, I shut my eyes and very slowly pulled my body away from the edge of the gate. I stood up straight and that's when I felt the light *thump* on the side of my left leg. It was my hand—somehow, my arm was still there.

One of the workers, a huge Scotsman, climbed up and brought me down. As he came close he looked at my arm and stopped for a moment, leaning over the rail to vomit. 'Don't look at it, son,' he said when he'd finished. 'Just don't look.'

Suddenly, I felt very faint and he grabbed me as I slumped forward, hauled me onto his back and carried me down. A small crowd had gathered by the time we reached ground level and I could see from the look on everyone's faces how bad my arm must have been, so I forced myself not to look at it.

Just then, Paul came running into the factory, took one look at me and said, 'Oh bloody hell.' I saw the colour drain from his face and his eyes refused to meet mine. He walked to one side of the room and rolled himself a cigarette. He came to the hospital with me in the ambulance and there an intern and a nurse stitched the ripped skin together, wrapped my arm in a sling and sent me home.

I was so pleased to still have the arm that I didn't think to question what they'd done. I was only fifteen and assumed the hospital and its staff knew what they were doing. It wasn't until about a week later that I began to think things weren't quite right. My arm was still wrapped in the sling position and it had started to smell. My hand had a greenish tinge to it.

It got so bad that Dad took me to see a surgeon in Perth who took one look and rushed me into hospital. There, a neurosurgeon and a plastic surgeon operated on me for nine hours. It seems a lot of the nerves had been severed, the elbow had been completely dislocated and there was even chook food left in the wound. Gangrene was beginning to set in, so had Dad not taken the action he did my worst fear would have been realised, I would have had to have the arm amputated. It turned out that it was only the flesh below my elbow that had saved my arm from being amputated altogether.

When I came round after the operation, the pain was excruciating. They had put a tube in my arm to drain away the fluid. That was bad enough but even worse was when they pulled it out of my arm. It was like having a piece of knotted wool pulled through my skin.

I ended up being in hospital for about a week, after which we were told I would probably never be able to use my arm again.

Not long after the accident, a guy I knew from work came knocking at the door. I couldn't get over the change in him. He'd been pretty awful to me at the factory but, being naive and gullible, I believed he now wanted to be friends. I felt really proud introducing him to Mum and Dad as my workmate; I hadn't introduced many 'mates' to them and I was so desperate to have a friend I overlooked what he had been like before.

He started taking me out to different places, like the beach and the park, and it took a while for it to dawn on me that all the things he suggested we do required physical exercise. It turned out that my new 'friend' had been paid by the factory to check out my injuries, to make sure that I wasn't faking.

Paul looked after me a lot in the months after the accident. I had to wear a plate on my hand so that my fingers wouldn't be permanently turned inward, and for a long time I had no feeling at all. Then, one day, as we were mucking around in the backyard, Paul threw a ball to me, and my left hand flinched as though to catch it. The excitement was so sudden and so fantastic we ended up screaming for Mum and Dad to come and see how my hand had moved.

It probably took about twelve months to get the feeling back into my arm. Endless sessions of physiotherapy and electromagnetic treatment eventually got things working pretty well. Even today, however, the skin on my left hand is very sensitive, and I can't completely straighten my fingers. I still have a huge scar right around the centre of my arm, like a mottled, flesh-coloured armband that stops just above the elbow, the thin strip of unmarked skin and muscle that saved my arm from being severed altogether.

Dad saw a solicitor about what happened but we didn't have a lot of money, and it was a huge company that ran the poultry farm. It was the same with the hospital that first treated me. With legal fees being so high, it just wasn't worth the risk if we lost. We were fairly simple people and the thought of paying huge legal costs for the rest of his life was just too daunting for Dad.

While I was convalescing, I spent a lot of time at Nan and Granddad's house, as they too had moved to Perth. Nan continued with the tradition of Oddfellows mints, and I spent many happy hours in her garden, helping her with the weeding. She grew beautiful sunflowers. They were huge and she'd let me pick the seeds from the middle, then we'd sit together and eat them on the back step.

Mum, Dad and us kids still moved a lot, different houses and suburbs around Perth. One place we moved to was further away, a lovely old house overlooking the bay at Albany. Albany was a strange place, nestled between two big mountains. Local legend has it that a monster—the West Australian Yeti—lives in the hills. Us kids were of course sure that we could hear it some nights, thumping around on the mountains.

The whaling station was still operating in those days, and from our verandah we would see the boats come in and moor the whales to pegs, ready to be carved up. It should have been idyllic looking down on the bay, but these scenes reminded me of images I had seen of Nazi concentration camps. Bodies being moved along and then stopping, standing still. Waiting. Death and stillness seemed to hang in the air. It was awful.

It felt as though every day I was witnessing murder, the butchering of those once majestic creatures. And as if that wasn't enough, the stench from the station filled the air and wafted up to our house. The loathsome, heavy, disgusting odour was a constant reminder of what was taking place in the sea. Those magnificent whales were no more than a commodity to be used for whatever purpose man decided.

Very little was wasted and they even ran a little gift-cum-tourist shop where people would pay to watch the destruction of the bodies that was the inevitable aftermath of the senseless slaughter.

I'm not a vegetarian, and I know that animals are killed every day for human consumption, but we don't queue up at abattoirs to watch. Imagine watching little lambs getting their heads chopped off—we just wouldn't do it. Yet for some reason, it was acceptable to watch the slaughter of whales. It was almost like paying to watch the Christians being thrown to the lions. I suppose that society hasn't really changed as much as we think it has.

I have never really been a political person, and I can't remember being aware of any campaigns at the time to shut the station down, although now I assume there probably were. I just knew I was witnessing something horrible and wrong. I couldn't comprehend how man could be so barbaric.

I used to go down to the jetty at night to fish for sweep, and one night I was sitting there when I heard a strange, melancholy sound. A baby whale, about the same size as me, swam past, calling and calling. It was eerie and heartbreaking; it must have been looking for its mother. Tears pricked my eyes as I realised the whale was an orphan, its mother chopped up for profit.

The dark green waters of the bay seemed to be full of huge sharks, attracted by the blood and guts of the whales. There were signs everywhere saying, 'Do Not Enter the Water. Sharks!'

There were news reports of a grey nurse or white pointer shark, measuring over five metres, prowling the area.

The TV news showed an aerial shot of the shark circling the bodies of three whales moored to pegs. It was swimming against the current, and took a bite out of one whale and still managed to push all three against the current, that's how strong it was. One of our neighbours, a little girl, went missing one day. The last anybody saw of her, she was doing cartwheels on the jetty, and everyone assumed the shark had taken her.

The shark actually put Albany on the map for a while. We heard on the radio that rock star Alice Cooper was at the airport. He had been touring Australia and had come to Albany to hunt for the shark. He'd kept the trip quiet until he was leaving, then practically the whole town rushed to watch as he flew away.

While we were in Albany Mandy had a boyfriend called Tony. He played guitar and told me he was putting a band together. He had heard me singing—in the shower, the car or somewhere—because I'd practise whenever I got the chance. Tony said the band was looking for a lead singer and suggested I give it a try.

Around this time my love for opera was causing me a bit of grief. I still sang my Mario Lanza stuff but I was starting to get picked on a lot. It was stuff like, 'You poof. You wanker. Why don't you sing some real music? You can't even speak the language, you idiot.' It didn't take much for me to get a complex and I soon learned not to sing the music I loved when other people were within earshot.

I suppose it's the same all over the world but, for me there came the growing realisation that Australians in those days hated someone who tried to be above themselves. Call it the Tall Poppy syndrome if you like but to them—and to me—it was someone who pretended to be something they weren't. And opera in particular was not the kind of singing people like me were, or should be, comfortable with. It was exclusive and elite, something only snobby wankers would have anything to do with.

Historically, of course, opera was performed for the masses, a play in which the story was sung. But as productions became more lavish, people felt naturally excluded by the language and the opulence. Production costs soared and so admission prices were high, with the inevitable and obvious result that it could be afforded only by the wealthy.

Fortunately, the situation has begun to change over the last decade or so. I would say that the first time the world was really introduced to what opera had to offer on a commercial level was when Luciano Pavarotti opened the World Cup in 1990 with 'Nessun Dorma'. Then the Three Tenors—Luciano Pavarotti, José Carreras and Placido Domingo—concert series began and underscored the resurging popularity of classical singing and opera. Now, classical singing has become a part of café society. Singers like the Three Tenors and, lately, Andrea Bocelli are heard everywhere, and the music not only of yesteryear but of history is accessible to everyone. Some of the more forward-thinking opera companies are even starting to perform the classics in the language of the audience, either because they have grown to accept the new pop status of opera or because they are finally accepting that you can't introduce people to something they don't understand.

But back in those days, as a sixteen-year-old living in Albany, opera was almost a shameful secret, something I could enjoy only when I was alone.

So I auditioned for the band and grew my hair long. I came up with a name for the band—Ash—and we practised in one of the portable classrooms at the local primary school. The first song I ever 'sang' with the band was the Black Sabbath number, 'Paranoid'. And talk about scream! I didn't sing that song, I screamed it, almost as loudly as that day I nearly lost my arm in the chook farm.

By this time, I'd spent a lot of my pop singing time impersonating ballad singers, but had never really thought about modern singers. So I started to do a bit of Mick Jagger and AC/DC. You name it, we did it. I was not yet seventeen when we got our first gig. It was at the local Albany High School, and I was scared stiff.

As it turned out, there were about a hundred and fifty kids there and they loved it. And, come to think of it, that gig and the way it went down was probably my first realisation of what I could do with my voice and what it could do to others. In a way, it was my first taste of power, of being able to emotionally move people with my voice.

Some wise man once said that power can be used for good or evil. It has taken me many years to realise that power isn't necessarily a bad thing. I have to say, though, that many of my experiences with powerful people had been negative—from the abduction, right through school with the bullying and even at work. Some of the scars, the physical ones anyway, have healed with time. But, to one degree or another, there has still been the emotional impact to contend with and it has taken me a lot longer to come to terms with. Today, however, I no longer feel uncomfortable or lost around people with power, people like the record company executives, tour promoters and others I have met. Their power—or rather my perception of their power—no longer intimidates me, instead it inspires me to greater things.

Looking back, however, I cannot say I felt anything but fear about power and what it could do. That is, until that night when, as a sixteen-year-old, I sang my heart out to a crowd of teenagers. I just knew that it was an inexplicable yet enormous buzz. I felt alive and whole. I was being Me. All those fears, those faltering insecurities, those dreadful frightened thoughts I'd carried around were gone. They simply disappeared up there on the stage. Up there I could be what I wanted—for a little while at least.

From that night on, I began to get a reputation as a bit of a rocker. It meant, though, that my dreams about being involved with classical music were put very much in the background, and I became even more guarded and secretive whenever I had the longing to sing that way.

So I bought an old guitar and practised for hours on the porch, learning the music of the Shadows and anyone else who was popular at the time. I would sit in my bedroom hour after hour, perfecting the notes and sounds of various singers, learning the words and voice inflections that I needed to bring a song to life. I loved the likes of Paul Anka, Neil Sedaka, Englebert Humperdink, Freddy Fender and Tom Jones. I even managed a mean Shirley Bassey. And everything I learned was by ear. To this day I can't read music.

Singing pop music and especially impersonating others became almost an obsession with me, and my life's ambition was to sound like as many people as I could. My passion for opera still burned deep, but I think at that time I tried to replace it with a new passion, one that was more acceptable and accessible. Any idea of singing opera professionally gradually became little more than a pipedream, largely because I knew it was ridiculous to think that an uneducated, poor kid with no background in traditional opera could ever actually be allowed to sing it. I thought I probably wouldn't have been allowed to listen to and see a performance even if I'd managed to scrape the money together to buy a ticket.

Even in Albany we continued to change addresses. From the house overlooking the bay we moved to a caravan park down near the beach, and then to a house in Mill Street. Dad got a job in the wool mills, where he operated a huge machine that usually took four men to keep going. It was considered a bit of an achievement, so much so that he got his photo in the paper for being able to run single-handed a machine that was about four metres wide and something like thirty metres long.

My arm had healed a lot by now, and Dad got me a job at the mill. Even though I could use my arm, there was a tiny delay, not more than a split second, between my brain and the action, so sometimes I would drop things or misjudge distances when holding things with my left hand. I was working on a spinning machine, feeding wool through rollers, when one day I rolled my thumb in with the wool. I don't know how to describe the pain that shot through my whole body. All I know was that the skin on that hand had become really sensitive as feeling gradually returned, so the normal pain of a thumb being crushed was magnified tenfold. Thankfully, the damage was eventually patched up, and I got a job in an antique shop, out of harm's way.

Dad bought me my first car when I turned seventeen. It was a Vauxhall Viva and we did it up together. I loved that car so much that I even used to sleep in it sometimes. Naturally, I got my licence as soon as I was old enough.

My next car was a Datsun 1200 that I bought on finance. I think I paid $2800 for it. I was only earning about $70 a week, so it was a lot of money. But to me it was worth every cent. It looked like a sports car, and with my first week's wages I bought myself a cassette player and created the perfect world inside my car. Wearing my Brut aftershave, I would listen to Cliff Richard and eat Cadbury's Coconut Rough chocolate. I knew without a doubt that I was cool.

It must have been around this period that Paul decided it was time for me to lose my virginity. In spite of the whole rock and roll thing, I was very naive and innocent when it came to girls. Paul, being Paul, took it upon himself to straighten me out. He was living in his own caravan and told me to come to his van one night, he had it all sorted.

I really had no idea what to expect. As I sat in that van I was torn between being horrified about it, and wanting to prove to Paul that I was a man. When I heard a knock at the door I opened it to see a very pretty brunette standing there. She probably wasn't much older than I was, but she seemed very sophisticated and worldly. Of course, I decided that I should try to act confident, as if I knew exactly what was going on, that I'd been doing this for years.

I really was incredibly gullible. I honestly believed that Paul would have kept his mouth shut and not told her that I was still a virgin. Not that it would have taken her long to figure out for herself, seeing that I was shaking like a leaf. There was a lot of inept fumbling on my part and, as I tried to cover up my innocence with a feeble excuse, she turned to me and said, 'Well, what do you expect for your first time?' That was it—any chance of anything happening was lost. Without going into too many details, the night was a disaster.

The girl and I actually became quite good friends after that and I often met her for coffee and a chat. Years later, my sister Mandy caught up with her and she told Mandy she often thought about me because I was one of the few men in her life who had actually liked her as a person, not for what they could get. When Mandy told me that, I was really glad that Paul's plan hadn't worked.

I had another experience not long after this that made me think I was cursed to spend my life as a virgin. I had managed to find a real girlfriend without Paul's help, a lovely girl. One night we parked at a lookout on a cliff above the town. One thing led to another, and I can remember thinking, *This is it, it's going to happen!*, when bang! I was jolted back to reality. I had parked the car at the back of the car park and been so caught up in the moment I hadn't realised the handbrake wasn't on. The car had slowly rolled forward. It had just reached the edge when my girlfriend grabbed the handbrake and wrenched it on. It was as if someone was teaching us a lesson for being naughty—we very quickly headed home.

Paul joined the army, but that only lasted for a short while and he was soon back with the family. He'd got married but that didn't last very long either. Then he met a girl called

Anna, a gorgeous little blonde, and became absolutely besotted with her. He fell madly in love with Anna, but her family was very involved with the Dutch Free Reform Church and did not want him around their daughter.

One night Paul asked me if I wanted to leave home. He knew that Anna's family would never accept him, so they had decided to run away together. I was an eighteen-year-old, non-smoking, non-drinking virgin, and I decided that it was probably time for me to leave the nest. So Paul, Anna and I packed up the Datsun and headed east, back to Shepparton.

## CHAPTER 5

## THIS TIME IT WAS DIFFERENT.

Our life had been a constant series of trips, always on the move. But for the first time it was us, the younger generation, who were deciding our destination. We had an absolute ball on the road. We'd all managed to save some money and I remember that trip as being so much fun.

We camped out in the desert a lot. Staring into the brilliance of the stars reminded me how very small and insignificant we were. I'd seen the sun set, followed by the twilight and then darkness many times, but now the experience seemed much more intense as my senses picked out the subtleties of change and the sights and sounds that belonged to the endless miles of barren earth at night to be replaced in their turn by the sounds and smells that belonged to the glare of daylight.

Senses dulled in the daytime become heightened at night; you can hear the shifting sand as a snake slithers by, the cracking of a twig as a dingo stalks its prey, the smell of food from a campfire miles away, carried on the desert air as if it was from a next-door barbecue. Sometimes we'd hear the throb and rhythm of an ancient sound and guess it must be some kind of ritual background music to the life teeming in the seemingly empty land. The rumbling of those distant corroborees reinforced and heightened the feeling that staring at the stars had given me. I was insignificant but at the same time part of something greater, something mysterious and yet to be discovered.

We were in no hurry to get where we were going. For me, it was more than a trip from Perth to Shepparton; it was a journey in which I was leaving behind my childhood and teen years and taking the first steps into adulthood.

When we arrived in Shepparton the fruit-picking season was still a few months away, so we went on the dole and stayed in the pickers' huts at one of the orchards in Mooroopna. Most of the big orchards there rely on transient workers during the picking season. To cope with the huge influx of pickers, orchards have huts, like little cabins, where the workers live. Fruit pickers are a diverse crowd, made up of students, overseas travellers, drifters and professional pickers who follow the seasons around the country.

The huts come alive during the picking season. Parties become part of the life as people from all over Australia and from overseas work and play together, sharing their sweat, their stories, their food and drink in the heat that can change from balmy to insufferable as the sun comes up and back to balmy when it goes down. Outside the seasons, the huts stand vacant and depressing, like a ghost town waiting to come to life. After the excitement of the trip, living in the empty huts and doing nothing soon got to us and I remember it as a very miserable time.

I think we went a bit stir-crazy. One day we were in the pickers' kitchen where Paul had spent hours setting up a war game he had bought called Panzer Blitz. The game was huge—spread across the whole dining table—and all the pieces, the mountains and soldiers and guns, had to be in the right place. It was to do with world domination and it could take up to two weeks to complete one game.

I have no idea what was said, but we started arguing and, like always with Paul, it soon got physical. Within minutes we were even throwing things at each other. Tempers erupted and I whacked him with a frying pan and he belted me with a chair. Things became so out of control that we both ended up spattered in blood from wounds to our hands, heads and other parts of our bodies. Paul, of course, had goaded me but maybe my part in it was all to do with pent-up aggression and a kind of perverse exhilaration that at last I was fighting back. Whatever it was, the ferocity got so out of hand I reckon we could have ended up killing each other.

Sometimes in life you do really stupid things, even though you know before you do them how dumb they are. This was one of those times. Looking back, it was like one of those scenes from a cartoon. The devil me was sitting on one shoulder saying, 'Do it. Do it', and the angel me was on the other saying, 'Don't. Don't.'

The devil me won, of course. This was one battle I was determined not to lose. I saw Paul's game sitting where he had painstakingly arranged it on the table and I tipped the whole thing over. Soldiers and tanks went sprawling around the kitchen and I took off like a shot out of a gun. That was the first time in my life I realised I could outrun my brother. I doubt I would be here today if Paul had caught me that night.

Anna and Paul were mad about each other, but I think at times she missed her family. She was quite religious and she'd looked for and found a Dutch Free Reform church just outside Shepparton. Paul and I drove her over there one Sunday and decided to go to the pictures while we were waiting for her.

For me driving around Shepparton didn't bring back any fond memories. All I could see were the places where I'd been beaten up. Sitting beside Paul as we cruised the wide, familiar streets that ran at perfect right-angles to each other, I looked out at all those places and couldn't stop myself shaking. All I could think about was those countless kicks and punches. It felt as though they were hitting me again and I wanted to be sick. And as much as I tried, I just couldn't rid my mind of the feeling that it would happen again. The fact was the more I tried to forget, the more painful it all seemed, and I just wanted to jump out of the car and run back to the safety and solitude of those abandoned huts. Paul could see how edgy I was and told me not to be so stupid. People grew up, he said, and it had been four years since I was there last.

We parked the car and walked to the cinema, and who should be sitting outside with his gang but Leo, the one at the very centre of the nightmare I'd been reliving only a few moments before. As I looked at him, time raced backwards. I was that kid again, fearing for my life. He was slouched against the wall, taking in the sunshine and joking with his mates. He was too busy chatting to notice me at first but then the fact that Paul and I had stopped and were standing motionless on the footpath must have triggered the thought that something was wrong. He looked up, mildly bewildered at first. As he raised his hand to his forehead to shield his eyes against the sun, his whole expression changed. It slowly dawned on him who he was looking at. He dropped his hand and, with his face no longer in the shadow, I could see it hardening as both his hands clenched into fists. The rest of the gang must have sensed it too because they all stared at Paul and me.

Tapping Paul's arm in some reflex warning action or simply to snap him out of it, I turned and started to run. I didn't know where to and I didn't care so long as it was away from Leo and his mates. Fear had pumped extra adrenalin into my legs and I found myself racing down the street, forgetting where the car was parked in my panic. Still running, I turned to see where Paul was. He was no fool and he knew that, as tough as he was, he couldn't take them all on. He was just a few yards behind me so I slowed down for him to catch up. He didn't say a word and just pointed. That was enough for me and we legged it to the car. Paul had the keys out before we arrived and frantically opened the door, jumped in, opened the door on my side and gunned the car into life. It kicked in first time and we sped off, the squeal of the tyres drowning out the screams and threats of Leo and his gang as we fled.

As we drove away I could see Paul was more furious than he was frightened. He hated being threatened and, even more, he hated coming off second best. I reflected later, that perhaps he was also feeling a bit protective, looking out for me.

Whatever he was feeling, the path of his revenge didn't dawn on me until about half an hour later. We drove out of town straight to a pub. As we approached it, the thought struck me that we might have just come out of the frying pan and were about to jump into the fire, because parked outside the pub was a long neat row of motorbikes, mostly Harley Davidsons. *Oh my God,* I thought as more fear piled on top of that which hadn't yet left me from the Leo encounter, *what the hell are we doing going into a pub full of Hell's Angels?*

But, despite the safety of the car, I wasn't going to stay outside on my own, so I followed Paul into the pub. Conversation stopped as we walked in. Blokes—huge and ugly blokes with beards and tattoos and dressed in leathers that looked as though they'd been dragged through barbed wire—stared at us as we stood in the doorway. Then, seeing we were no threat and without a word being said, they turned back to their drinking and talking as if we no longer existed.

I kept my mouth shut but Paul shouted something, a name perhaps, above the noise and, as if annoyed at the intrusion, they turned towards us again. Then one of them moved forward and, with a glint in his eye, reached out his hand.

'G'day Paul,' he said and, behind the beard and the scraggy long hair, I could just recognise the face of one of the kids we used to hoon around with in our budding bikie days. He and Paul shook hands. He looked at me and, smiling at the stunned look that must have still lingered in my eyes, told us to join him for a beer. It was a command, not an invitation, and I hurried to the bar for what suddenly became one of the most welcome and refreshing beers I've had in my life.

Paul chatted with him for a while. I just stood there trying very hard to be invisible. Not even Paul wanted to hang around too long so, after a few more beers and hand-shakes, we left. Paul told me when we got in the car that I wouldn't have to worry about Leo any more. I don't know what happened after that, but Leo never did bother me again.

It was around this time that I decided to go on a TV talent show called *Star Quest*. It was a locally produced show that aired on GMV 6, and it was compered by a man called Jeff Valance. I auditioned and got on. I sang 'Please Release Me' and won my heat, so I made it to the grand final. For some reason I changed from Englebert Humperdink's melodious ballad and chose the more raunchy and punchy Tom Jones classic, 'Delilah'. It was a mistake. The song didn't worry me, and I loved singing it, but it just didn't suit my voice. Either that or I was a bit nervous because it wasn't a great success.

Still, I had a great time doing it, especially with the big production background that went with it. It was given that soaring big-band treatment. Singing and being part of the whole thing was like a little taste of stardom—just enough to keep the dream alive, though not enough to make it a reality.

We had been living in Mooroopna for a few months when the rest of the family came over from Perth and set themselves up in an orchard in East Shepparton. So we moved there to join them. By this stage the family had grown a bit as Mandy was now married to Tony and had a baby.

Anna's folks found out where she was through their contacts in the church and asked her to visit them in Perth. We thought she went home to explain that she and Paul loved each other. But she didn't come back; she stayed in Perth with her family.

Paul was devastated. He had no money so he hitchhiked all the way across the Nullarbor. When he got to Perth he didn't get to speak to Anna. Instead, her brothers got hold of him and beat him up pretty badly. They told him that if he ever saw her again, or even tried to see her, they would find him and kill him.

He never saw Anna again. Losing her changed him completely. But on top of the hypocrisy of what her brothers, the churchgoers, had done to him and the fact that he must have been heartbroken at losing the first girl he'd ever loved, there was an even crueler irony in store. And it wasn't until years later that we discovered it.

It happened when my singing career started to take off in 2003 and ABC television featured me on *Australian Story*, which went to air nationally. Among the hundreds of emails and letters we received afterwards was one from Anna's children. Not long after Paul finally left Perth she had given birth to his twins. And they had been trying to track him down for years.

As it was, Paul arrived back from Perth and, even though he was battered, bruised and emotionally devastated, he was at least back with the family.

Mum and Dad seemed to have settled down too and

they caught up with a few old friends they had made while living in Shepparton before. And one of the couples they met up with again were the parents of my first girlfriend, Mary-Anne.

I was keen to see her again, and I probably had more on my mind than hand-holding and kisses. Her family was living in a house at one of the local orchards and I was quite excited about visiting her although I did wonder whether her annoying little sister, Jeanette, was still around. She'd been a geeky little drop-kick who'd always managed to butt in at the wrong time, just when Mary-Anne was coming round to my way of thinking.

Time, of course, changes a lot of things, and I'd certainly altered since going to Perth four years before. I was no longer a gangly, spotty teenager and my body had developed into a younger version of my father's—wiry and strong from manual labour. As was the fashion in the late seventies, my hair was long and I had grown a moustache to signal approaching manhood.

But, while I knew I was different now, for some reason when I knocked on the door of Mary-Anne's house I expected nothing to have changed. Certainly, her mum looked the same as she opened the door, and I half expected to see Mary-Anne looking just as she had, sitting at the kitchen table.

'Mary-Anne's married,' her mum said matter-of-factly, smiling kindly as she noticed my disappointment. Then, almost as if to console me, she said, 'Why don't you go and see Jeanette? She's down the hall in her bedroom.'

Not wanting to be impolite, especially to such a nice lady, I trudged down the hallway. I'd say hello to the little drop-kick and get out of there as quickly as I could.

I knocked on the first door I came to. 'Come in,' a voice said. It wasn't Jeanette's, it couldn't be. As I opened the door and looked in, I immediately went to close it again, thinking I had the wrong room. Sitting on the bed was the most beautiful girl I had ever seen . . . long blonde hair framing a delicate pixie face, skin as soft as milk and eyes so warm they blended perfectly with the gentleness of her smile. I was so stunned that I felt my face redden, suddenly and uncontrollably, and I mumbled my apologies and went to shut the door.

'Hello Peter,' she said softly. I literally couldn't speak. I simply stared into the beautiful blue-green eyes of this gorgeous girl smiling up at me. And, as I stood there, with my jaw obviously hanging somewhere around my chest, she laughed. 'It's me,' she said, 'Jeanette.'

I must have stood at that doorway for a whole minute. And that's all it took for me to fall completely and utterly in love.

## CHAPTER 6

'A WHIRLWIND ROMANCE'...

that's how you could describe Jeanette's and my courtship. I had never felt so happy or complete in my life. We were both still in our teens but neither of us had led sheltered lives. We had already become young adults by the time we met.

At eighteen, I had been earning a wage for years and had never had a traditional upbringing in the sense that many kids of my age had. For her part, Jeanette had been expected to work hard in the orchards from the time she became a teenager. So neither of us had the luxury of planning careers or 'finding ourselves' on overseas trips before we went to university. Ours was a typical working-class life. Other than this persistent, niggling desire I had to sing, our expectations were a product of our environment.

All of that might have been the cause of it or it might have been something inside both of us that wanted to get out and away from what we were—if only for a little while—but almost from the outset my relationship with

Jeanette was passionate and intense. For the first time in my life I allowed myself to trust someone outside the family.

I had never felt comfortable with intimacy and was still a virgin when Jeanette and I met. But that had little to do with my inadequate fumbling in a caravan or leaving the handbrake off in a car park. Sex had come into my life violently. It had been horrific, frightening and inexplicably painful. At an age when most kids are being reassured that their nightmares are only dreams, the worst kind of nightmare had for me become a reality. From that moment on, the idea of sex had become synonymous with pain, humiliation and unfathomable fear. Intimacy and the warmth of another body close to mine was something to be shunned.

But with Jeanette I learned that making love to a woman is the most beautiful form of human expression. I was completely besotted with her; a whole new world had been opened up to me and I wanted it to last forever. We were very young, and I think young love can be the most intense and passionate of all—when it is free of the cynicism that comes with so-called maturity and when the very newness of the emotions being experienced makes it all the more exciting. I can remember thinking that I was the first person to feel this way, that it was only Jeanette and I who understood true love.

And so it was that at eighteen my life took a completely new direction. The family continued to move around. Mum and Dad lived for a while in Moonee Ponds and then Ascot Vale, so Jeanette and I stayed with them and I got a job working in a factory with Dad. They then moved on to Warrnambool, and Jeanette and I went to Bright to work on a tobacco farm.

Those early times with Jeanette were so happy. Anyone who has ever been in love will know that wonderful feeling of all-consuming passion. When you are not with the person, all you do is think about them. When you are with them you can't believe they love you, that you are worthy of their love.

My self-confidence had never been high, and all the negative thoughts I had about myself had been reinforced time and again at school with the bullying and the humiliation. I'd never had a close friend, so for me falling in love with Jeanette was not just about a man loving a woman. It was learning to trust someone who was not related, who didn't love me just because I was family. Jeanette was not only my lover, she became the best friend I had never had, the person I could laugh with, share my hopes and secrets with, the person who made me feel safe and wanted.

Living in Bright was a real adventure and the man we worked for was very kind to us. He gave us a caravan to live in while we were waiting for the tobacco season to start, although I soon learned that his kindness came at a price.

There were loads of chestnut trees growing around the tobacco farm and every year the owner looked forward to making a tidy profit from their nuts. But, just before the chestnuts were ready to pick, rosellas would come down from the hills and virtually demolish his crop. One day I was sitting outside the caravan with Jeanette when the owner approached and handed me a gun and ammunition.

'I want you to take care of the bloody parrots,' he said. 'They're ruining the nuts.' He spoke in a broad Italian accent, and left no room for arguing. Still, I knew I had to try because the thought of killing those beautiful parrots was awful.

'Sorry, I can't do it,' I replied. 'Isn't there something else you can do?'

'What do you mean, you can't do it?' he said. 'I give you a place to stay. I give you food. You have to do it. Those bloody birds could cost me thousands of dollars.' With that he handed me the gun and walked away. I knew he was right. I had no choice.

It was one of the worst experiences of my life. As those beautiful, brightly coloured birds came soaring in, chattering and squawking excitedly for their evening meal, I stood there and picked them off. I can remember crying as I loaded up buckets with their carcasses and walked back towards the farm.

Looking back on that dreadful carnage, I know it is one of the experiences that have shaped the person I am today. I truly believe that there is nothing worse in life than to be forced to do something that is against your nature, or to be prevented from doing something that is part of who you are. The violence and the cruelty I have been exposed to have contributed to my undying pacifist nature. And in their own sick and perverse way, those very experiences I'd encountered became my inspiration to vow that what I hated and feared most would never become part of who I am.

Perhaps that was why I found so much solace and inspiration in the beauty of opera. Songs I loved were easily accessible to me. My endless hours of practising meant that to hear opera, all I had to do was sing. Yet everything about my life told me that the *world* of opera, that place where I truly felt I belonged, was inaccessible. If I could not stand up for what I believed in against a tobacco farmer, how could

I ever hope to find the strength and the courage to tackle the obstacles ahead of me in forging a career in opera?

To take the life of another creature for nothing more than profit seemed so wrong to me, yet there I was, doing as I was told. That evening, I felt like a murderer carrying my buckets of feathered bodies back to the farm. As I passed by the other caravans on the property, a door opened and a huge Yugoslav man called me over. His face lit up when he saw what was in the buckets, and as he took them from me, he invited Jeanette and me to his van for tea that night.

We stood outside his van and watched over a bottle of wine as the plucked carcasses of the rosellas were roasted over a campfire. Strange as it might sound, it didn't really bother me to eat the birds. Call it a contradiction if you like but I think my conscience was salved by remembering those words of my father's: *Never kill something unless you are going to eat it, son.* Perhaps that made the meat seem a little sweeter. Whatever, the meal we ate that night was delicious.

I suppose the wanderlust of my family had also become part of me because Jeanette and I moved around a lot. After the tobacco farm we picked fruit in Silvan and Monbulk, and lived for a time with Mary-Anne and her husband on a share farm just outside Benalla.

Mary-Anne's husband, Wayne, was an odd sort of bloke but with an inspired, even clever, touch to some of the things he did. The owner of the farm, for example, told us to do something about the starlings that were eating his crops. I had no idea how we could get rid of them, but Wayne put his mind to work. He went into town and bought a load of mousetraps, set them among the crops and waited for the starlings to land.

Another time Wayne decided that he was going to make his fortune catching wild parrots and breeding them. He made an ingenious trap that caught them without doing them any harm. He soon had quite a flock which he planned to keep for a while, until they calmed down, and then sell them. Unfortunately, he housed them in a disused chicken shed. They contracted a disease and all of them died.

For all his ingenious ways, though, I always felt a little uncomfortable around Wayne. I never quite knew what he was going to do next, so after a while Jeanette and I decided it was time to move on.

Mum and Dad were still living in Warrnambool with the rest of the family at a caravan park, so Jeanette and I joined them. Then we moved to Simpson, a little town between Colac and Warrnambool where we got a commission house. The whole family ended up working at the local cheese factory, and I remember that time as being very happy and settled.

From the moment Jeanette and I started together I'd been convinced life could not have been happier. The birth of my daughter proved me wrong. I stayed with Jeanette throughout the whole labour. She was going through her own hell and, as any father who has done it will agree, there's an overwhelming feeling of utter uselessness as you have to stand there and watch the person you love endure so much pain. But then, as though by magic, there is another person in the room, a person who exists only because of you.

I looked at this tiny, pink little person and loved her completely and totally from the moment I laid eyes on her. I can remember unashamedly and proudly crying tears of joy as I held my beautiful daughter for the first time.

Jeanette and I were married not long before Sally was born in March 1979, but then something happened. It wasn't sudden, and it wasn't there and then in that hospital ward, but a change came into our lives. It was so imperceptible neither of us noticed it. Not at first at least, but it grew.

Jeanette was just sixteen when we had Sally, and living in Simpson did not offer any real diversion from the daily grind of motherhood and looking after a home. I had never really had a traditional childhood and, having left school so early, had spent most of my teens either working or recuperating from the accident with my arm. So I couldn't relate to the things Jeanette was missing. At sixteen, at a time when most girls her age were worrying about what to wear at the local disco, the poor kid was stuck at home with a baby in the middle of nowhere. And a 'poor kid' was exactly what Jeanette was.

I was blissfully happy. We had a nice house, a healthy baby and, for the first time in my life, I felt really settled. I was the one in charge of my own destiny. I was no longer at the beck and call or the mercy of my parents' constant need to keep moving, to keep searching for that perfect place. I had created the perfect place. I had found my own family and at last I had found a home. Perhaps I was a bit egocentric and maybe even a bit selfish as well, but I was so happy, I assumed Jeanette was too.

Then one day I came home from work and sensed something wasn't right. I sat Jeanette down and asked her if there was anything the matter, whether Sally had been playing up or whether there were any problems around the house, that sort of thing. I was shocked when she looked at me, a mixture of frustration and hardness in those lovely eyes, and told me she couldn't stand living in Simpson any longer. She was going crazy with boredom, and needed to be around more people. So we moved.

We packed up and shifted to Colac, which was not far away. It was a typical Australian country town—laidback, easy-going and friendly but, like many country towns, riddled with social and emotional problems beneath the surface that were allowed to simmer until some kind of crisis cried out for a solution. But, as quiet as it was, compared with Simpson it was a thriving metropolis.

We moved to a caravan park out of town, and Jeanette soon made friends with a group of local girls. Our life took on a kind of routine. I worked during the day, and most nights she went out with her girlfriends to the local pubs or the disco while I stayed home with Sally. Jeanette seemed a lot happier in Colac, and so I was happy.

I hadn't done much singing since I'd been with Jeanette, but at the caravan park I began to sing again. I was a bit older now, and didn't care so much about what people thought. And I would sing my opera songs in the shower, or as I was pottering around looking after Sally. As you can imagine, it was quite loud in the confines of the caravan, so I started slowly and quietly and then, when I realised that I wasn't getting picked on any more, I let it become louder and found I was becoming more confident with it.

I knew Jeanette's friends thought I was weird, fluffing around looking after a baby, singing opera, but I didn't care.

I had learnt over the years to adapt, to find happiness even in the most awful places and situations. So I would often sit outside the caravan in the evenings, waiting for Jeanette to come home. I'd feed bread to the possums and stare at the stars, and I created a happy world with what I had.

There was a local theatre company in Colac, and one day I went in to see if I could try out for their next production. They were putting on a play called *Finian's Rainbow*, and they needed a red-haired tenor who could speak in an Irish accent. My ability to mimic extended to accents, and I think the organisers nearly fainted when I assured them that I could manage an Irish one 'to be sure, to be sure', and launched into a rendition of 'Serenade'. Of course, I got the part. I also did a bit of singing at a local Carols by Candlelight production where I sang a gospel song called 'Somebody Bigger than You and I'.

So once again I lulled myself into contentment, adjusting my world to fit in with my idea of happiness. I was singing again, this time the music I loved—or at least close to it—and my wife seemed to be happy with our life.

Mandy and Tony had decided to head back to Perth, and it was probably after they left that I began to realise there were problems in our marriage I couldn't ignore. It seemed the more I tried to please Jeanette, the worse things got. I can see now that as she tried to pull away to have her own space and establish her own identity, I tightened my grip on her. So she struggled even more. I don't want to assume anything on Jeanette's part, but I think perhaps she was trying to find out what she wanted in life. I couldn't understand what she was going through since I had everything I had ever wanted. Maybe in Jeanette's case, she hadn't yet worked out what she wanted. But, whatever it was she did want, she was becoming increasingly sure that she didn't want me.

For some reason she decided we should follow Mandy and Tony to Perth. Thinking this might be what she was really looking for, I let myself think it could be the thing to solve the problems that were building between us. After all, when our family had been in crisis years before, moving to Perth seemed to have brought Mum and Dad back together. So I was feeling really positive as we packed up the car and headed off, ready to begin a new life together.

Now when I look back on that time in Perth, I remember it as one of the darkest, most painful periods of my life. It soon became apparent that Jeanette no longer loved me; our marriage was a cage she was trying to escape from. The night she told me it was over I was in shock, I could only watch as she packed her things and prepared to leave.

The one thing I had always been able to rely on had been the unity of the family. Through all the tragedies and triumphs, the family had remained solid and dependable. It seemed unthinkable to me that my little family would break up. I sat stunned, unable to conjure up any words that would make her stay. Then I noticed that Jeanette had begun to pack for Sally.

'No!' I said. 'Not my baby. You're not taking her!' It was probably one of the few times in our relationship I had stood up to Jeanette. I was confused, angry, sad and unable to think clearly, but I knew without a doubt that I would never let her take my little girl.

Jeanette looked at me. Perhaps something in my eyes told her that this time I meant what I was saying. Perhaps she felt relieved. She was just a kid herself and to be on her own with a baby must have been a frightening prospect. Whatever it was, she stopped packing for Sally, picked up her bag, turned and walked out of our lives.

We were living in a second-floor flat at the time. As I stood on the balcony watching her leave, I decided I would jump. The pain and hurt of losing her was just too much. Then I heard a cry from the bedroom. It was like having a bucket of cold water thrown over me and I knew in that moment what was really important in my life.

I sat holding Sally for most of the night, like a frightened little boy clutching his teddy bear, comforting myself as I rocked her backward and forward. I had nothing—no money, no wife, a crappy car. But as I looked at my sleeping daughter, I knew I had everything. It was time to return to what was safe and dependable, so I packed the car to head back east to Mum and Dad. Still in a daze, I don't think it had sunk in how completely my life had changed in that one evening, and all I wanted was to feel safe again.

I didn't realise that night that things would get a lot worse before they got better.

## CHAPTER 7

## ONCE AGAIN I WAS ON THE ROAD,

only this time was like no other. A lot of that trip in 1980 is a blur now. I hurtled east with Sally in the back, barely able to see through the tears.

It was one of those situations in life where my reality was apparent to me, yet it didn't seem real. I couldn't comprehend that I had been so wrong, that the woman I loved so much didn't love me. One of the songs on the radio seemed to sum up what I thought were Jeanette's feelings towards me. It was Meatloaf's 'Two Out of Three Ain't Bad': 'I want you, I need you . . . but there ain't no way I'm ever going to love you . . .'

I'm sure anyone who has been through a time of great emotional pain can name a song that seemed to encompass their feelings. The same can be said of great joy, and for me it often seems that it is through music that I can truly experience the depths of passion, whatever that passion might be. Music allows me to explore the dark memories in my soul that might otherwise remain hidden.

Unlike the earlier trip across with Paul and Anna, I found no joy or comfort in the desert. Perhaps your senses depend on your heart. I was flat and empty and alone, feelings accentuated by the miles and miles of desolate landscape I sped through. I know that it was only the presence of my daughter that stopped me from running the car off the road and ending the pain once and for all. It would have been so easy to just turn the wheel towards an approaching power pole or a road train coming my way. I have often wondered how many poor souls have taken that option.

I kept going, however, heading back to what was safe and comfortable, the need to be with family becoming more urgent the closer I got. Had Sally not been with me, I would have stopped only for petrol, but I needed to get nappies and food for her. On about the second day I pulled into a little town just outside Kalgoorlie. I think the police noticed me before I saw them.

Looking back, I can understand why they took the action they did. They saw an unregistered, unroadworthy car with bald tires being driven by a deranged young kid with long hair who looked as if he hadn't slept for days. And in the backseat was a baby.

I don't think I was actually arrested and I certainly wasn't put in jail. But I was taken to a hotel room and held for about a week while the police determined who I was and what the situation was with Sally, who was put into temporary foster care. And that was when I learned that even at your lowest point, things can always get worse.

Seven days alone in a hotel room with no idea of whether I would see my daughter again. Seven days to sit

*Top left*: Me as an 18-month old in Leeds, Yorkshire, 1960. (Note the curious stick holding the pram still!)

*Top right*: 'Dreamers'—Mum and Dad, somewhere in Sydney, around 1966.

*Centre left*: Mum holding me, aged 4, and Mandy, aged 2½.

*Centre right*: Near Terrigal in 1967—Dad, holding Josie as a baby, and Mum, with me, Mandy and Paul in the foreground.

*Left*: At a park near Sydney—(back row, left to right) me aged about 7, Mandy 5 and Paul, holding ball, 8; (front) our cousin Bindi, and my sisters Josie, 4, and Sarah, 2ish.

*Above*: Paul aged 7, Mandy 4, and me, about 6, in Sydney.

*Below left*: (from left to right) Sarah, me, Mum, Dad, Josie and my younger brother Jamie, just hanging out. Looks like we've been swimming.

*Below right*: Me, aged about 16 1/2, and Mandy, about 15, just before we left for Albany.

*Above*: At my black stripe grading, executing a twin front snap kick. My friend Brett Holbrook is on right. (Photo courtesy of *The Standard* newspaper, Warrnambool)

*Below left*: In Warrnambool, Victoria, when I was about 25. I look happy with myself because I had just received an A grading in martial arts.

*Below right*: Lisa, lovingly biting my lip! She was born in July 1988.

*Above*: Great sound, great guys! As a band Limited Edition was so successful, we were together for eight years and played twice a week, almost without fail. (From left to right) Me, Peter Bird the bass player, Joe Willis the guitarist and singer and Phil Lawrence the drummer.

*Below*: Trying my hand at mixing! Ern Rose (on left), me and Hadyn Buxton at Metropolis Studios in South Melbourne. The 'ghost' in the top right corner is Margaret Orr, keeping us under control!

A promotional picture for my rock-and-roll band work taken just after I took over Evergreen Shoe Repairs in Hawthorne in 1997. (Photo by Veronica Bromley, my lovely friend)

*Above*: Alan Jones giving me a singing lesson! This was the night we first met, at Nick's home in 2002. With us is Kris Messara. The back of the head belongs to Vladimir Vais.

*Below*: (Left to right) My babies—Lisa, Sally and Cathy—on a photo shoot for a magazine.

*Above left*: Denis Handlin, CEO Sony Music, taking me under his wing.

*Above right*: Kate Ceberano, me and my sister Mandy at Ron Barasi's testimonial at Telstra Dome in Melbourne. That night I made my first 'classical' stage appearance, singing 'Credere'.

*Below*: Lisa (on left) and Cathy (on right) with their mum, Sharon.

*Right*: In full flight at a Diabetes Foundation charity night in the Paladium Room at the Melbourne Casino.

*Below*: A post-concert speech and CD signing at Sydney Opera House in May 2004. With me is Margaret Orr, who accompanied me on my CD *Boots And All*.

and think, to grieve and to worry, to cry and try to exorcise my private demons. I was totally alone. I had lost everything I valued in life and the despair I felt became palpable. For that week I became nothing. My identity had been ripped from me and I struggled to cope with the totality, the utter completeness of how alone I was. I was a wifeless husband, a childless father, and a son who just wanted to be home.

Words cannot describe the emotions I went through in that room, staring at the brown brick walls, thinking the worst and hoping for the best. As the days merged into each other, I lay on the bed and cried, the loss too great to even acknowledge. Life really is odd, isn't it, and the perspective of it can hit you at the oddest times. Such as the fact that before the police came into my life I'd thought the worst that could happen was that I would be left alone to raise my daughter. Now that was the best I could hope for.

Throughout my time in Kalgoorlie, the police and officials were kind and considerate. Maybe they could see I was telling the truth, but they obviously had to check out the facts for themselves. Only a week had passed since I had stopped for those nappies, yet it seemed like a lifetime. I'd barely eaten and if I looked a bit suspect when the police first picked me up, I dread to think what I looked like at the end of that week.

Then, after all those days of waiting and wondering, there came a knock on the door. It was the sergeant who had been good to me, and with him was a man formally dressed in a suit. My immediate thought was that a detective had been brought into the case, that this whole thing was going to get even worse. I felt like a condemned man, sure they were to arrest me for kidnapping Sally. Then the sergeant introduced the other man as the head of community welfare in Western Australia.

It was only then that I noticed a woman standing behind the door holding my daughter. In a soft voice the man in the suit said, 'We've finally made contact with your wife, and she assures us that what you've told us is true.' He smiled as I wrapped my arms around my daughter, stunned. For a moment I couldn't believe that they were giving her back to me. But there she was and all I wanted to do was hold her.

'We've also contacted your parents,' he said. 'They'll be waiting for you when you arrive in Colac.'

He told me they'd sold the car for scrap and within the hour the police had taken me and Sally to the train station. There they gave me the money they'd made from selling the car and two one-way tickets on the Indian-Pacific. We were on our way home, back to Mum and Dad.

Yet again I found myself travelling across the Nullarbor under the canopy of the stars. Instead of the childhood noises of my squabbling brothers and sisters, I listened to my own child in her fitful sleep. I sat and quietly played the harmonica, the night stars witness to my pain. I was so lost in my own world that I failed to notice the crowd of passengers who had gathered to hear me performing, their appreciation one of the few positive memories of that painful journey. As so often happened in my life, performing showed me that my passion for music was powerful enough to move complete strangers.

Mum and Dad had moved again, of course, but the location wasn't important; I felt I was home because I was with them. They were living in a house at Scott's Creek when we arrived, so I got a caravan and Sally and I lived at the back of the house for a while before we moved into a flat at Timboon, just the two of us.

That whole episode, as I say, was for me a time of great darkness. I was lost—emotionally, spiritually and physically.

Lessons learned early in life stay with us and the coping strategies we develop as children tend to be the things we return to at times of great stress. I had watched over the years as my family kept itself together by constantly moving. We would simultaneously run *from* one place or situation *to* another place that was better, where the promise or hope of a better life waited.

I would never intentionally apportion blame for what I am or for my actions on anything that happened when I was young. But the choices we make are often a result of what we have learnt, even if the lessons show us the futility of our choices. I had watched Mum and Dad struggle for years, and come to know that happiness can't be found by running, and least of all at the bottom of a bottle.

But perhaps I wasn't looking for happiness after the loss of Jeanette; perhaps I just wanted to dull the pain. One thing I know for certain is that I wasn't coping. I began to experience panic attacks and in otherwise normal situations I'd feel my heart palpitating and my breath becoming constrained. I would feel that the world was closing in on me and I was going to die. My body seemed to be reacting physically to the emotional stress. I, the non-smoker, the non-drinker, began smoking and drinking heavily, trying to hide from the questions that had no answers, trying to run from the reality of my life.

The one thing I have never questioned is the love I feel

for my daughter, even though there were times when I felt I was merely going through the motions of being a dad. Again I can look back to lessons learned early in life when, throughout all the many problems Mum and Dad had, they remained good parents. They never once made us children feel unloved or unwanted.

And so it was now, at the lowest point in my life, that Mum became my rock. She was there for me, supportive and helpful in practical ways, a grandmother trying to be Sally's mum.

As I sank deeper into depression, I began to question my life, to try to make sense of the way I was living. I had always had a sense of something greater than myself and I remembered back to the time when, as a little boy, I had found that magic in those *min min* lights along the road to Darwin. And then there was that equally magical Mario Lanza song, that had awakened in me a longing for something more, something beyond my reality.

Through the haze of alcohol and sadness, my mind kept returning to those moments in my life, moments that had meant so much to me. But there were also moments that remained unresolved, like the abduction, that stayed with me and remained as intense as the day they happened. That was when, as a young adult, I became a small boy again and, if only in my head, I was alone again with a monster and begging for my life.

I had carried within me so many conflicting emotions, issues that were never resolved as a small boy, and they had continued to impact on my life into adulthood. But above all there was that time when I was a child in Terrigal.

The enormity of what had happened in Terrigal became unbearable. I was no longer able to hide from the insecurities hidden deep inside. So many emotions that should never be felt by a child so young had stayed with me. Many people say that they have no memory of great trauma, that it is hidden so deep that it is never acknowledged by the conscious mind. Sometimes I wish that was the case with me. But what happened to my sister and me that day has been burned into my memory, and has played a huge part in shaping the person I was to become.

I was close to eight years old and Mandy was nearly six. It was the last day of term and we were both excited as we walked home from school. Like most kids we were looking forward to the holidays, but I was particularly excited because it was one of the few times that we had actually finished more than a few weeks at one school.

I had done some paintings in class and I was so proud of them I couldn't wait to get home to show them to Mum. I had also made her a little pottery snail and I was looking forward to seeing her face when she got the presents.

We passed a car on the side of the road and then we heard a voice call out to us. 'Hey, can you kids show me where the beach is?'

I pointed in the direction of the beach and said, 'Yeah, it's just up there.'

I looked into the car and saw the man had a map on his lap. He looked at me and said, 'I'm new in the area, do you think you could show me and I'll take you home to your mum and dad. I'm a friend of theirs.'

Of course, I wasn't smart enough to think to question him further, but I'll never forget that it was Mandy who said, 'Peter, no. Let's go.'

We had grown up in an environment where people came and went and strangers became our friends in a short time. So I thought Mandy was being stupid. The whole world was our friend, after all, so why shouldn't we trust the people we were with? 'Come on,' I said. 'Let's get in.'

On seeing us move towards him, the man said, 'I'm only going to take you just up there,' and again he asked us to show him where the beach was. I must have hesitated and perhaps something in my mind told me that it was a strange request. Even to a little boy of my age, it was pretty obvious where the beach was.

He noticed my hesitance because he changed his approach. 'Listen kids,' he said, 'I'm a friend of your mum and dad's, they've asked me to drop you home.'

We'd moved so many times that short-term friendships for our parents were nothing out of the ordinary. And a car held no fear. It was our comfort zone and often it had been our home.

It was also a long walk to our place and, with the stuff we were carrying, a ride seemed like a good idea. One memory that stays with me to this day though is that Mandy didn't want to get into the car, but with all the insistence of a big brother I persuaded her, and pushed her in first.

Some details about that time are clouded. I don't remember now what type of car he drove, for instance, or even what the man looked like. I know that we sat on the front bench seat and I think it must have been some sort of panel van or an enclosed station wagon.

I do remember every detail of what happened in that car. We drove off and, as we passed the street where we lived, the nightmare began.

We began to tell him that he had missed our street. Just then he removed the map from his lap, exposing his erect penis to us. Although we were probably more street-wise in many ways than other kids, we were actually very sheltered and modest within the confines of our family. The only penis I had seen in my life was my own little boy's doodle, so this thing looked like a monster to me. But it wasn't just it or the size of it. It was the whole mood of the man that seemed to fill the car, threatening and angry, yet weirdly hopeful and cajoling. It was a strange atmosphere to be part of and neither Mandy nor I had any idea of what was going on. But we knew we were in danger. I can remember thinking, *Okay, we're going past the beach, we're not going home and this huge thing is being shown to us.*

Both Mandy and I were saying, 'Please take us home, take us home.' But all he would say was he was just taking us for a bit of a drive.

I have never told anybody exactly what happened in that car, and I am not going to be explicit now. I think it is enough to say that the confusion, terror and the pain were worse than anybody can imagine. I was only a kid after all, and had no idea at first about what I was seeing him do to my sister. All I knew as I looked in horror at her little face was that he was hurting her and making her cry and vomit.

My fear turned to anger, and I started screaming at him to stop, balling my hands into little fists as I hit him and tore at his arms. But it meant nothing to him, and all I could think of doing was to scream at what I knew was frightening and painful and wrong. Through the fear and panic, the strongest way to describe what I felt was pure heartbreak, watching my poor little sister being abused by this man.

Suddenly, he pulled out a knife and held it to my face. I knew that he meant it when he said he would kill me. There was my sister kneeling at his feet on the floor and all I could do was sit there in terror, feeling absolutely helpless. He grabbed me by the scruff of the neck and threw me over the front seat to the back of the car, where I sat on the floor listening to my sister sobbing.

Then I started to beg, 'Please, please leave her alone. Please stop hurting her. I'll do anything for you.'

As difficult as it might be to conceive that a little kid, begging for the life of his sister, might be able to think through his panic, I remember a thought coming into my head. And even today I can still remember using the words, 'I'll do it.'

I didn't really know what I was agreeing to do. Had I known I might not have offered myself in Mandy's place. But it would have made no difference anyway. He went on to use both of us in turn in what seemed to be one long, long day, although apparently Mandy and I were missing for three or four days. In reality, it might as well have been five years because what happened in that car that day and in the days that followed was to affect the rest of our lives.

But, as one hour melded into the next and neither night nor day mattered any more, it dawned on me that the only way our nightmare was going to end was when he killed us. And I had no doubt that was what he intended to do.

But then, as I looked down yet again to where Mandy sat on the floor in front of the man, I looked at my paintings. They were the most valuable thing I had. I was so proud of them, they were the first thing that I had really achieved at school. I can remember thinking, *I know, I'll bribe him*. I honestly thought in that moment that he would trade the paintings for our lives. He had finished with Mandy for the moment, and that's when I spoke up. 'If I give you my paintings, will you let us go home?'

I sat there and watched as he picked them up and looked at them, one at a time. I still remember hoping, as he studied each one, that he would like them all; that I had done a good enough job with them. At that moment something happened to his face. And that was when I saw a tear in his eye. In that moment he stopped being a monster. He became a man. He looked almost fatherly as his eyes moved first to the paintings and then to us. Mandy was cowering on the floor. I managed to catch her eye and signalled for her to hush. I knew that he was considering what to do with us.

He took my paintings and rested them across his lap, as if holding on to them with his two hands helped him think. Finally, he looked at us and said, 'Get out, before I change my mind.'

The gratitude I felt towards him was overwhelming. I still kept thinking that he would change his mind and kill us, but the sheer joy at hearing those words was too much, and over and over again I kept saying, 'Thank you, thank you, thank you', as we got out of the car. I was so overwhelmed that he was letting us go, that it was almost as if I was thanking him for the ride.

He drove off with my paintings, and left us standing there.

It was almost dark by this time. Mandy could barely walk, so I half carried her as we made our way towards a house that had its lights on. In the back of my mind I still thought that he would change his mind and come back for us.

We got to the house and knocked and as the door opened we both screamed at the man who stood in front of us. All I can remember thinking was, *Oh God, another man*. As soon as he saw us he started crying. He knew who we were straight away, our photographs had been all over the news. He yelled for his wife, who wrapped us in a blanket as she told us her husband would drive us to the hospital.

The police were waiting with Mum and Dad when we got there. Mandy was admitted immediately.

Between the tears and the hugs I can still remember my father's face. He was always a gentle, loving man, but with his realisation of what had happened, the look on his face was something I'll never forget. It was a mixture of anguish and rage, and I know without a doubt that he would have killed the man who had hurt his babies.

The next few days are a bit of a blur. I got to ride in a police car with Dad as I tried to retrace where the man had taken us. We went down one bush track after another. They all looked much the same to me. It was pretty scary, going to all the places the man might have taken us, but the police wanted me to do it while it was still fresh in my mind, and, piece by piece, the picture came together.

Whatever I did must have made a difference. About a week later, the police came to our house and showed me a photograph. Over the years I must have shut the image out of my mind because I have no recollection now of what the man looked like. But I remember looking at his picture and seeing a fatherly face looking at me. I didn't see a monster, I saw the face of the man who had liked my paintings.

Dad has never been a big man, more wiry, but I looked

up at him and his chest seemed to expand as though it was about to explode and, without saying another word, he took off out the door. I followed in the police car as he ran all the way to the police station where they had the man in custody. Standing next to Dad in the station I saw the look of hate on his face again, but this time it was mixed with desperation. He begged the sergeant for five minutes alone with the man. As he pleaded, both he and the sergeant had tears in their eyes.

The sergeant looked at Dad and said, 'Sorry mate, it's more than my job's worth.' Then, probably as much to ease Dad's pain as to show him rough justice had been meted out already, he took him to the cells and opened a door. Dad looked in at the man. He had obviously been beaten pretty badly. I don't know who did it but I don't think it made Dad feel any better.

The man ended up being sentenced to ten years in jail, but apparently he was paroled within two years.

Not long after Mandy came home from hospital we were on the move again. We probably would have moved anyway, but it wasn't easy living in the town after what had happened. Not only were the memories still fresh in our minds, we also had to contend with the stares and taunts from others. Kids would yell out things like, 'So, you've had sex, Brocklehurst. What's it like?'

I suppose this was to be expected, as kids can be incredibly cruel, but the adults were just as bad. We were walking along the street one day when a couple of women started pointing and I heard one of them say, 'There go those sex kids.' To me it sounded weird and confusing, as if we were members of some kind of club or something.

Today, as I piece together those moments in the car, I am increasingly convinced there are many truths to the way a man behaves, some of them brutal and unpalatable. And one of them is that, whether it is through remorse or guilt, the strongest moments of clarity for a man are after he has reached orgasm. Truth is revealed after making love. What happened in that car had nothing to do with love, but I do think now that at the end the man was thinking clearly, that somehow in that moment we touched his humanity. I truly believe to this day that no matter how evil a person is, there is humanity somewhere in everybody. At the time, I merely thought he liked my paintings.

As for me, I don't think any person ever gets over an experience like that. It becomes a part of who you are, and shapes the way you live your life. I developed a complete lack of trust in men: anyone from outside the family was considered with suspicion, and it is only in the last few years that I have been able to trust men enough to form friendships. For most of my life I have turned to women for friendship.

At one stage I even hated my own masculinity. I found it very difficult to separate overtly masculine traits from dominance, or predatory behaviour. To me they were one and the same. I have also spent a lot of my life trying to prove that men, myself in particular, aren't offensive or something to be feared. Nothing would horrify me more than if I was to intimidate or frighten someone by virtue of being a man.

Over the years I have dealt with these truths about myself when I have been at my most vulnerable. All the years of bullying, knowing I was different but not being able to comprehend how or in what way. The only thing that did become clear to me was that I was unlovable, that Jeanette had sensed something was wrong and that she hadn't loved me enough to stay. I had been carrying the guilt over making Mandy get into the car ever since it had happened and I began to think that I was bad, that I had done something wrong to deserve this.

So it was that after my marriage broke down, so did I. I became consumed by negative thoughts that developed into a vicious cycle the worse I felt, the worse my life became, and so I felt even worse.

Though I had always turned to women for friendship and support, now I found myself mistrusting women as well as men. I felt alone and lost and drifting, trying to make sense of a senseless world where bad things happened to little children and no one was to be trusted.

I reverted to a childhood habit. I began to run again. Running from the pain and uncertainty, running until my head swam and I was gulping for breath. I pounded along under the stars at night, pushing my body until the physical pain matched the pain in my heart.

It was a night filled with stars when I finally came to rest and looked up, tears streaming down my face as I searched the sky for something, some reason or meaning to my life. And that was when I experienced what I can only describe as a spiritual awakening.

As I stared up into the vast nothingness, suddenly everything became clear. The abduction, my marriage breakdown, my life, everything that was causing me so much pain didn't matter. I felt part of something greater, some bigger picture, a humanity that lasts forever. Somewhere deep within me, through all the despair and misery, I had found hope.

I won't say I found the meaning of life, but for the first time I realised that I should stop questioning, stop looking for answers that could never be found. True faith is to believe without question, and that is what I discovered that night. From that time on one level of my life changed completely. Emotionally and physically I was still a wreck, but spiritually I began to feel strong.

I had found a way out of the lowest point in my life. I began to read the Bible and issues took on a new perspective and clarity. I was finding the strength to deal with the traumas that had guided my life. I was able to incorporate the bad with the good and make choices about who I would become.

We all have choices in life, of course, and while what happened to me is now a part of who I am, to a large extent I like to think I have chosen how I have dealt with the pain. I don't blame the past for the mistakes or regrets I have in life. We are given a life and what we make of the challenges along the way is up to us.

Mandy is a counsellor now. She helps other people deal with their own emotional pain and trauma. I think we have both found an inner strength that we may never have tapped into had that awful thing not happened to us. Of course it was far too high a price to pay, but I have tried very hard throughout my life not to be bitter and not to let myself be eaten up by the experience.

Sometimes I can look back on what happened with a kind of detachment, as if I am watching two children who happen to have the faces of my sister and me. There is no way to truly impart the horror of what happened to anyone else, but I have tried hard not to let it consume me, to not let myself become bitter and nasty.

If I was to meet that man today, I think I would say to him that I can never understand how a human being can do that to another human being. One of my old bosses used to say to me, 'Don't ever look back unless you can gain from it in the future.'

I would tell that man that I despise him for what he did to us, and more particularly what he did to Mandy, but that we had become the people we are today, in part, because of what he did and what happened. Two things have stayed with me from that experience. One is the relationships I've had with other men, the years of loathing and lack of trust. And yet the other is that, no matter how bad things get, I truly believe that good can always rise above the bad. We all have it within us to conquer evil, sometimes we just need to be shown how.

That night when I ran myself to exhaustion was pivotal to my life. I had reached my lowest point and was given the strength to climb up, to reach for something better. I won't say now that I was conscious of making any life-changing decisions, but I do think that from that night on I realised where my true passion lay. My love for Jeanette, as total as it had been, was gone. In my search for meaning and passion I had felt empty and alone for so long, but after that night I returned to my comfort zone. I came back to what had kept me safe as a child.

I began to submerge myself in music once again. My voice has been described as remarkable and I feel that I can acknowledge this without seeming big-headed or boastful.

That's because I believe my ability is God-given; it is something that I was born with and which has developed over the years. Maybe it is similar to the ability of a sportsman or an intellectual. Some people are born with a talent or skill that burns within them, that they just can't ignore. It is then up to that individual how they use that talent and whether they develop it to its full potential or ignore it and let it lie dormant.

Throughout my time with Jeanette my passion for music had been overshadowed. Now I turned back to what was within me so that it might help me get through my loss. It was through being true to myself, to who I really was, that I found the strength to move forward and put the past behind me. Not just the immediate past, but all the sadness and pain that had followed me from childhood.

CHAPTER 8

## THERE IS A DISTINCT AND BUSY BAND SCENE

outside of Melbourne. It is a culture in which musicians
from towns and provincial cities come together and
perform in the various country pubs and clubs. Warrnambool is a large regional town servicing the western district
in Victoria. It is quite a beautiful city built on the hills overlooking the Southern Ocean, and most of my family had
settled in the area around this time. I moved with Sally to
live with Mum and Dad again in a sleep-out at the back of
their house in a suburb of Warrnambool called Winslow.
After the darkness of my marriage break-up I began to
submerge myself in music.

A local band called Working Class Hero was looking for
a lead singer. I auditioned and got the job. We did well-
known covers and originals, and got a lot of work around
the clubs and pubs. Once again I had something positive in
my life to hold onto: I was singing and the response I got
was great.

Performing on stage brings with it an almost magical allure. I was to find out pretty quickly that, had I been so inclined, I would have no shortage of women willing to sleep with me. Women would actually come up to me after a gig and tell me they were in love with me. I now think of these women as lost souls trying to inject their own lives with a little of the magic and excitement they saw on stage.

Still battling with the fallout from my marriage, I found myself mistrusting women as well as men, and all the baloney about 'loving' me only hardened the way I felt. Of course they didn't love me, it was just my voice and possibly this bloke they saw on stage.

The few times I did try dating, I soon knew it was point-less. After all, the real me, the one who lived with his parents and was raising his daughter, was nothing like the image I projected. So it wasn't long before the women I dated ran away, angry with me for shattering their fantasies of what life as a 'rock star' was like. This was driven home to me every time I mentioned my daughter. They couldn't get away from me—the real me—quickly enough.

I learned to live with the contradictions. At night on stage, singing songs of love and heartbreak to people who saw me as a success, my voice moving them enough to offer themselves to me, by day a man trying desperately to be both mother and father to a little girl, living alone at the back of Mum and Dad's house.

Although we had a fairly good following around Warrnambool, I began to get a bit frustrated with the band. Anyone who has worked around that scene will tell you there are two types of musicians. There are those who have a full-time job and play as a hobby. For them it's a chance to unwind, much like a game of golf or a fishing trip. Then there are the serious musicians, those who sacrifice a steady income and even a normal family life to pursue their dream of making it, of playing music full time.

Of course, I fitted into the second category. I was burningly ambitious and, because of that, I must have been a pain in the bum to work with. Near enough was never good enough for me. The music was everything and I wanted us to be as professional as possible. While the rest of my life was in a shambles I wanted the one thing I was good at to be right. So when I was offered the chance to join a more professional band with really great musicians, I jumped at it. I still feel a twinge of guilt at leaving Working Class Hero when I did, as I know I left the band in the lurch, but I was offered a chance and I took it.

The new band was called Skyline and it had a good reputation around the area. They were more commercial than Working Class Hero and were interested in recording originals. I think I was searching for recognition, for fame even, and added to that perhaps music was my escape from the life I was living. With little education, I just couldn't see any other way out.

And there was the passion. It was still there and it had become so insistent and so consuming I had to force myself to take stock, to give myself a reality check. Opera and the music of the classics were still there, deep down inside me. I thought that one day I might be able to spend the time and rekindle that dream, but in the meantime, if I was to give myself half a chance of making it, I had to be realistic and brutally honest with myself. The way to that goal would have to be through contemporary pop and rock music. So

I persevered with what I had, not content by any means but at least doing something I enjoyed.

It was around this time that I was accepted to compete in a well-known television talent show. I did well in the first heat and got through to the grand final. Excitement and nerves danced together in my stomach as the day approached. It was almost surreal to be in a television studio again.

I sang my song, the Lionel Ritchie hit 'Hello', and got the biggest score since a very young Johnny Farnham had appeared on the same show years before. The buzz around the studio was palpable. The winner of the grand final was to be given a cheque for $10 000 and, for singers, there was the offer of a recording contract.

Taping a show like this does not happen in the hour we see on screen; the performers are recorded and then watched by the panel of judges, who give their score in a separately taped segment. Performers were asked to appear out of breath, as though they had just finished their performance.

I waited around the studio all day, with crew members and other contestants coming up and shaking my hand, congratulating me on a great performance and wishing me well for the future.

I was clearly in the lead when the final act, a tap dancer, came on at the end of the day. She did a competent dance routine and smiled at the camera, and two of the judges scored her accordingly. Then they got to the third judge, a very well-known celebrity. He gave her the highest single score ever recorded in the history of the talent show. I was beaten by one point.

For a few hours I had believed that it was about to come true, that all the hopes and the years of dreaming were to be a reality. If that judge had stood in front of me and kicked me in the stomach, I would have felt less flattened, less shocked by what had occurred. I, like thousands of Australians, had admired this man for years. I couldn't believe he had done this to me.

It turned out that I wasn't the only one shocked by his decision. When the show went to air there was such an outcry that an inquiry was held by the television station. The tap dancer was actually this judge's niece. Had I not scored so highly perhaps the discrepancy would not have been so apparent. Not long after this the show was taken off the air—but that was no consolation prize.

So I continued with the band, doing the pub and club scene around Warrnambool, working all hours at night and looking after Sally during the day. The band had a good following and I started making a bit of a name for myself.

Working in a band is a fairly intense sort of atmosphere. Rehearsing, performing and creating music can bring members together as a tightly knit group. But the intensity has two sides; sometimes close friendships are formed, but at other times creative differences can lead to jealousies, antagonism and even hatred. In some ways it's like a sporting club where others judge the hours of practising and rehearsing.

The reaction when you play live to a crowd is immediate so, unlike other jobs, you know straight away how successful you have been. You never have the luxury of having an 'off' day and you can't hide, so this pressure to perform, and to perform before others, adds to the passion. But throw in jealousies and egos and you have something volatile and, with precious personalities in particular, it can explode.

At the same time there is also the added intensity in the need for everyone to get on. The band shares so much and the range of emotions includes a kind of blokey culture. This I avoided. It wasn't a prudish thing, but I never really came to terms with the sex and drugs of rock and roll culture. It wasn't a judgmental thing because it didn't really matter to me what they did. But it might have been that I couldn't rid myself of the thought that singing with the band was merely a means to another end, so I wasn't interested in the drugs and sex. And for that I suppose I was thought of as a little strange.

I had grown used to being considered an outsider, so I didn't think it odd that even in an environment where I was successful I still didn't really fit in. I was there for the music. That was what was important to me and it was all I cared about.

It had probably been about eighteen months since Jeanette had walked out of my life when I met a woman who seemed different from the others. She hung around after gigs. Maybe I had become the one who was different and perhaps, when she came into my life, I was ready to move forward instead of looking back. She was a friend of one of the guys in the band and often came to see us perform. It took me a long time to work up the courage to speak to her; I had built a wall around myself and didn't know if I was ready to trust someone again. But one night after a gig we got chatting and ended up going to the beach where we sat on the sand, listening to the breaking waves and talking. We sat there until the sun came up. I felt so comfortable with her that I let myself go and we talked about everything. Slowly, as we spoke, the thought crept into my mind that maybe, just maybe, there was hope.

It was around this time that one of the band members asked me to do lead vocals on a song he wanted to write and record. We worked on the song together and recorded it in a studio underneath a row of offices in Warrnambool. Warrnambool is quite hilly, and the offices were on the slope of a hill. Underneath were cellars, and a local musician called Peter Bird had turned one of them into a studio. We could only record at night, so as not to disturb the office workers. After all those years of listening in awe to the voices on our record collection it was an exciting time to be actually making a record with my own voice.

We would rehearse our numbers in a music shop run by one of the band members. One night the girl I was falling for turned up there. I was so pleased to see her I smiled as I walked towards her. Then I saw her face. She looked so cold as she stared at me, I couldn't understand what was going on.

'So, you like the thought of my family's money. That's what you really find attractive, isn't it?' She spat the words at me with such venom that it took me a while to collect my thoughts. Then it dawned on me. Her family were quite wealthy and well known in the district, and she had got it into her head that I was some sort of gold digger. I must have sounded pathetic as I stammered that I had no idea what she was talking about.

'Just leave me alone,' she said, looking at me with such pure hate I couldn't believe this was the same girl I had shared such a special night with on the beach. Then she smiled sarcastically as she motioned across the road. 'You should stick to girls like the one in the chicken shop', referring to the girl who worked in the chicken shop opposite who had hung around and listened as we rehearsed. Why had she changed so much towards me? My life had just begun to turn around, I had my first real friend in the guy I was doing the single with and I was allowing myself to look to the future. But, as I soon found out, the trust I had allowed to surface was all a lie. I was fooling myself again.

And it all became painfully clear shortly after that night. I was driving along, listening to the local radio station, when I heard a familiar voice. The DJ introduced the guy I had done the single with, who was with another bloke, and the two of them were talking to the DJ about the single *they* had made. They played the record and there was my voice, coming out of the car radio. Then the DJ asked them who had done the vocals and they told him, 'Some guy called Trevor Brocklehurst.'

Trevor! What the hell were they talking about? I couldn't believe what I was hearing. My head felt about to explode as I began to realise what was happening. My mate—my best friend—had used me. I turned the car around and drove straight back to Warrnambool to the music shop, where I knew he would be once the interview finished.

The anger, the hurt and probably everything else that had happened over the years welled up inside me. Perhaps I was angry at myself as much as anyone else, at having let my guard down and allowing myself to be made a fool of. Whatever it was, I was seething when I got to the shop. And on seeing my 'friend' I raced up to him and grabbed him by the throat screaming 'Why?! Why?!'

He looked at me with utter contempt. 'You got your fifty bucks, now piss off,' he said.

The night we had put down the vocals, I had been paid

fifty dollars for the session. Things were pretty tight for me financially and so, when I was offered the money, of course I took it. This meant I didn't have a leg to stand on. I was considered a session singer and that was the end of my part in the project. The only recognition I got was to be listed last on the record label. And it ended up going to number seventeen on the local charts.

It also turned out my so-called friend and recording partner had been the one who started the rumours about me being a gold digger. He fancied the same girl and could see she preferred me. Maybe this was the reason he cut me out of the record deal, I really don't know. I do know that at a time when I was beginning to rebuild my life, it felt as if the rug had been pulled out from under me yet again.

CHAPTER 9

I HAD NO TROUBLE GETTING GIGS

with other bands. I played with Mod Squad and Underfire
and my life continued on as before, doing the pubs and
clubs, singing songs of love to drunken crowds and especially to the women and young girls who were blinded by
the lights of the stage.

But while I sang and got on with living, I knew I had to
put that wall back up. A person only had to be nice to me
and I considered them a friend, so to protect myself against
my own gullible nature I had to make sure at least part of
me remained shut off, but how much I don't know. I felt
myself becoming a loner, a recluse, holding in my thoughts
and feelings and bitter not only at others but at myself for
being so stupid and exploited. The indifference I'd felt
toward the women who hung around the band turned to
contempt, but not even that was as much as the contempt I
felt for myself. I couldn't respect a woman who actually liked
me, because I believed myself to be unlikable.

Among the sea of faces that came to see us perform, one that stood out was that of the girl from the chicken shop. Some nights when she'd finished work she would stand around outside the music shop where we rehearsed. While I didn't really study her I couldn't help noticing in her face that familiar look of not knowing why she was there but, at the same time, of longing to be part of it. The noise, the fun, the music and the few moments of magic it all brought with it. I also saw in her what I was.

*You should stick to girls like the one in the chicken shop.* Those words the other girl had spoken that night of the recording session kept coming back every time I looked across the road and saw the half-smiling, half-longing look on the girl whose life seemed to revolve around the band at night and cutting up chickens during the day.

Often, after doing a gig, I'd get in my car, alone, and drive up to a lookout to watch the ocean waves crashing on the shore. It was my way of finding a mental bridge between the music, the crowds and the stage on one hand and real life on the other. Just like when I was a child, and I stared at the ferries in Sydney, I found solace in watching the beauty and mystery of the tides and the sea.

One night, as I sat with my thoughts, I heard a car pull up. A door opened, and I heard someone inside say, 'Go on, go for it,' before the car sped off. I looked across and saw a girl standing there, clutching a can and looking unsure of what to do next. It was the girl from the chicken shop. I knew what was coming next and I winced inwardly.

Since I joined the bands I had become accomplished at untangling myself from the arms of drunken women. Sex could never be like that, or even a casual thing, for me. I know to a lot of people it might sound strange, but I have never had a one-night stand. I was in an industry where the opportunities and temptation were probably ten times as great as most men face. Perhaps things would have been different had my life been different, but they weren't. And besides, a drunken woman smelling of cigarette smoke just doesn't do anything for me.

So I wound down the window of my car and asked, 'What are you doing? What do you want?'

She hesitated, obviously a little shaken by my tone of voice, and muttered, 'They threw me out.'

I let the silence hang there for a while and then, whether out of pity and a kind of empathy for the way she must have felt after what someone had done to her, or simply because I too could do with a bit of company, I half whispered, 'Come on. You'd better get in.'

I expected the worst but to my surprise I couldn't detect the familiar smell of alcohol. Then I saw the can the girl was clutching was nothing more than a soft drink. She looked up at me and, staring back at her big eyes, I thought of a startled deer.

'Sorry. That was my sister and some of her friends trying to be funny,' she said. 'I'll leave you alone.' She spoke softly and as I continued to look into her eyes I realised I'd been wrong. She was no more than an arm's length away from me but she hadn't even reached out to hold on to the door as I opened it. She'd simply stood there, quite still. Then she turned to walk away, shoulders slumped, and I could feel her embarrassment and shame at being dumped on the side of the road like a piece of trash.

'Hang on,' I said. 'You can't walk all the way back to town. I'll give you a lift.'

She stopped and lowered her head. Finally she looked up and said, 'I'm Sharon.' Then she smiled, reached out for the door and with a sigh so slight I could hardly hear it, she eased herself into the seat beside me.

From that night on, Sharon and I would meet after gigs and go for drives. For me it was the company, a brief escape from the isolation that I'd built for myself. And it helped that the sweet gentleness she'd shown me on getting into my car that night became more a part of her. It washed over onto me a little and I told myself that perhaps she was a bit smitten with me. She'd never had a boyfriend and there was me, the epitome of the long-haired rock star. She probably thought I was a real man of the world. How wrong she was!

We never really dated. Instead, we got to know each other slowly and gently. For me it had to be that way. I still had to come to terms with trusting another person and— more to the point—trusting my own ability to have any affection for others. But Sharon never pushed me. I told her a little about myself and the way I felt and she let me take things at my own pace. It wasn't long though before we became what you could call a couple or, as others might say, an item.

I met Sharon's family and saw straight away that her gentle nature came from her mother, Anita, who was one of the loveliest people I had ever met. She had managed to raise eight children by herself in one of the roughest commission suburbs in Warrnambool. But none of it, nor the struggles she'd overcome in the rest of her life, had made her bitter or even sorry for where she'd ended up.

Even so, some of Sharon's family were wary of me. In fact it would be fair to say some of them didn't like me at all. First of all I was a Pom, and the term 'Pommy bastard' wasn't always used with affection. Also I don't think they'd met anyone like me. They reckoned I was a bit arty-farty and not blokey enough. Although on the surface our backgrounds might have seemed similar, in reality our lives had been quite different. I came from a family that didn't swear, particularly around women, and I found it a bit confronting to be around people who used language whenever it suited them, regardless of who might be nearby.

Still, not all of Sharon's family were hostile and I got along with some of them really well. As time went on, I found my place within the family and eventually I got used to their way of talking to each other. Sharon ignored their reservations about me and told me to do the same.

I still had times when I was unsure, not only of myself but of what was happening around me, when I would question whether it was for the best. So one day I decided that it was time to put our budding relationship to the test.

From the moment they met, my daughter Sally and Sharon got on like a house on fire. They immediately warmed to each other and, as their friendship grew, one of the great joys Sharon had was brushing Sally's hair. And it was times like these that this strange lump I felt in my throat managed to calm the turmoil of my thoughts.

It had been so long since my daughter had known the love of a mother. Sally was four years old by this time and one day after Sharon left she looked up at me and asked, 'Daddy, is that my new mummy?' I knew there and then that we had to become a family.

Not long afterwards Sharon moved in with Sally and me. We stayed for a while with Sharon's family before moving to the Fig Tree caravan park just outside of Warrnambool. Sharon worked during the day and I worked at night and so life settled into something of a routine. As well as my regular band gigs, I began freelancing as a singer and found that I had no shortage of work.

One of the guys I met in the band scene was called Damien, and one day he asked me if I wanted to do a record with him. Despite what had happened before, I wasn't about to walk away from a chance at making it, so we wrote a song together called 'I'll Never'. The B side of the single was actually a song that my brother Paul wrote the lyrics to, called 'I've Found the One'. This time I was determined to learn from my past mistakes, so I made sure that I had acknowledgement on the record.

We recorded it at Peter Bird's studio, tucked beneath the buildings on the main street of Warrnambool. We had almost finished the song, but I felt that something was missing; there was more that could be added.

'It needs something. I can almost hear the sound I want, something haunting. Like the old sax that used to be so popular in the fifties.' I was thinking out loud when I caught Peter looking at me with a strange smile on his face.

'You need to go to the old drive-in theatre,' he said.

I must have given him a look that told him I thought he was mad, but he just laughed. 'I reckon you'll find what you want at the drive-in.'

I couldn't resist a good mystery, and I knew Peter was not going to tell me anything, so I set off to the old drive-in theatre, not having a clue what I was going to find. It was pouring with rain by the time I got there, and the place was a bit eerie, with all the old speakers standing silent in the dark. The only light I could see came from the dilapidated projection room, so I left the car and walked through puddles to knock on the door.

'Who the bloody hell's that?' I heard the sound of shuffling feet and something falling, then the door was opened just enough for me to look down at two bloodshot eyes.

'My name's Peter Brocklehurst. I need a sax player and Peter Bird said that I should come here,' I said. The words came out in a rush. I could sense that the door was about to be slammed in my face as I stood in the rain.

The man looked me up and down and then opened the door wider to let me in. The sour smell of stale alcohol hit me as I followed his shuffling figure into the room.

'I don't play sax any more,' he said, sitting on a bed that was almost hidden among the debris, and then I noticed the black and white photos that lined the walls. A man was smiling at the camera, sax in hand, alongside all the stars I had grown up admiring—people like Normie Rowe and Johnny O'Keefe. I looked at the figure on the bed and couldn't help but feel pity for this once-talented musician, living the life of a hermit with only his fading pictures for memories.

His name was Barry Shields, and I stayed for a while and chatted about music before leaving him alone with his thoughts and his alcohol. As I drove home that night I couldn't get the image of this man from my head. I wondered how many other people with real talent had given up all hope of a 'normal' life to chase the elusive goal of stardom. And when they reached that goal, how many managed to stay there, up in the heights that most of us only dream of?

I couldn't shake the feeling of sadness. Perhaps it was not only that someone with obvious talent had fallen so far, but maybe it was a glimpse at my future, of what chasing a dream can do to your life.

We were at the studio a few days later and I was feeling very down. The meeting with Barry had really affected me, and we still had what seemed like a blank hole in the middle of the song where a lead break was needed. Then there was a knock at the door. Peter opened it and Barry Shields walked into the studio. He nodded in my direction and walked to the sound booth, where he put on the headphones and listened to the song. Then without saying a word, he opened his case, took out a tenor sax and started playing. We sat spellbound, unable to speak or move as the most beautiful sound echoed around the studio. When he had finished, he packed up his sax and got ready to leave. The only exchange of words I can remember from that night came as he passed me—he shook my hand and said, 'Good luck, son.' Then he left.

We never saw Barry—or Bazza as he was known professionally—again. A few days later he was found dead at his drive-in hideaway. Apparently he had suffered a massive heart attack. I have always felt grateful and privileged that such a talented man contributed to the music we were creating that night. To this day the single we recorded remains one of my most treasured possessions, as it was the last time the magic of this great musician was heard.

Finally I had achieved something with my music, and now it was time to get airplay for the song. This proved a lot harder than we imagined, and was a lesson that talent alone does not guarantee success in the music business.

People often forget that music is in fact a business—even if you have the best voice in the world, you won't get very far without some business acumen. No one will. And therein lies the importance of a manager. It just cannot be under-estimated. While you might have the voice, it's the manager who sorts out the quagmire of wheeling and dealing that goes into promoting a record.

We didn't have a manager, so we were relying on that other great provider of fortune, luck. For some people, good luck does just seem to happen, but the luckiest people I know have had a hand in how luck shines on them. The single had been out for a while and was getting no airplay on the local radio station, even though we had quite a name around the area.

Warrnambool's music scene was very strong at that time, and quite a few well-known artists would come from the city to perform. One day I heard that the singer Kamahl was in town, and a bit of calling-in of favours meant that I was able to meet him one night after a gig.

I was really nervous as I went to the pizza restaurant where I was to meet him. I got there at about eleven o'clock and my heart sank when I saw the loads of people milling around outside. I was sure that I would be thought of as just another fan looking for an autograph. I got to the door and gave my name, and was quite shocked when the owner of the restaurant let me in. I was ushered to a table at the back of the room, and there he sat, surrounded by people who seemed to be hanging on his every word.

I don't know what I expected that night. My experience

on the talent show had taught me that not all stars are the same as their public personas. I was beginning to think of those who were well known as being in a different place to the rest of us mere mortals, almost like being in a twilight zone from which they rarely ventured out into the real world. We saw them all the time on television and in magazines, but they weren't the sort of people you would bump into in the local supermarket. I used to dream for years of finding the key to the door that would allow me access to the zone, so that I would belong with these special, talented people. But I knew this was just a fantasy, they were untouchable, and just occasionally we were allowed access to them. Then they would disappear again, back to their own sphere.

So it was with some trepidation that I sat down next to Kamahl. He was known to millions of Australians for his deep melodic voice, and I was a nobody, a singer scratching out a living in pubs and nightclubs. I half expected to be ignored, and I don't think I would have felt any animosity had he treated me that way. I was really surprised when he turned his gaze to me and began to ask me about myself. I sat with this lovely, gracious man for ages, talking about my life and experiences as a singer, and he seemed genuinely interested in what I had to say. I left the restaurant that night feeling on top of the world; it had been wonderful to share a conversation with someone who had reached the top of his profession.

I had to come down to earth the next day. I might have been allowed into the rarefied sanctuary of a star for a few hours, but the reality was that I was a singer who couldn't even get his record played by the local radio station. Kamahl had told me that he was being interviewed by the local station, so as I drove along I tuned in to hear what he had to say. The DJ began by talking about the thriving local music scene that existed in the district.

Then Kamahl's beautiful deep voice with the slight accent filled the car and I couldn't believe what I heard him say. 'Well, that might be right, but I don't understand why your radio station doesn't do more to support local talent.'

The DJ sputtered a response and I nearly ran the car off the road at what I heard next.

'I met a young man last night, Peter Brocklehurst, and he tells me that he can't even get his single played by your station.'

I had created my own luck.

From that day it seemed our single was played non-stop; I found it hard to escape the sound of my own voice. We eventually went to number twenty-two in the local charts. I remember that time as being a real buzz; doing promotional work and getting a higher profile was to give me a slight taste of what it would be like to really make it, to be somebody.

For a time I was living an almost schizophrenic life. Sometimes I was a rising star, about to make it big in the music scene, but for most of the time I was struggling to make ends meet. I had to make a choice about my priorities: the reality was that I had a young family to provide for, and pursuing some pipedream seemed selfish and wrong.

I was one of thousands of young men hoping to make it in the entertainment industry, and I knew in my heart that the struggle was a lot harder than many people thought. Sharon and I were married by this stage, and it was a time when we needed to start settling down and building for the future. The choice I had to make seemed pretty clear to me. I could continue to pursue what many considered to be a future based on fantasy, risking rejection and failure. My experience on the talent show and then with the first record had taught me that I was a very small fish in a pool of sharks. My other option was to go with what I knew was steady and strong.

Family had always been my shelter, had always kept me strong even in the most difficult times. I had almost lost my family once before. Now that I had been given another chance at happiness, I wasn't about to let it go.

# CHAPTER 10

## SHARON WAS STILL WORKING

in the chicken shop when her boss approached her one day and asked whether we would be interested in buying a chicken shop he had in Hamilton. Neither of us had ever run a business before and my only experience with chickens had been when I nearly lost my arm in Perth. But this seemed like a good opportunity to make a real go of our lives, and it was far more tangible than pursuing a singing career. The figures looked really promising, and running a business of our own would mean that we were in charge of our own destiny. We didn't have any money, so Sharon's mum put her house up for us as security on the deposit and we made the move.

What had started with so much enthusiasm and excitement soon became a disaster. The business was being run on an overdraft which seemed to go up and up the longer we went on. It didn't take us long to realise we just couldn't make ends meet. The figures we had been shown were based on a trading period where a lot of specials were sold, so the takings looked a lot better than they really were. To make any sort of profit we had to raise the prices and this meant we lost business. We were working eighteen-hour days with nothing to show for it. Because we had bought the business on vendor terms, if we missed one payment the owner had the right to come in and take the shop back.

We worked so hard in that bloody shop, but ultimately we had to be realistic and call it a day. We were just getting further and further into debt. What had seemed at first to be our way out became our captor; we were a slave to a business that was leading us nowhere. The worst thing to come from that whole experience was that Sharon's mum Anita lost her house. While the rest of the family understandably turned against me even more, Anita was so supportive and kind that, before the bank moved in and sold the house, she even let us stay with her for a while.

The whole episode made me feel terrible because I had failed Anita, the one person who had believed in me. Once again self-doubt began to haunt me.

Sharon and I needed money so when a job was advertised at a Mister Minit key-cutting/shoe-repair shop, I applied. I got the job and began my training as a shoe repairer. Although I was too old for an apprenticeship, the company ran courses on different aspects of the business, and I found I had a bit of a knack for cutting keys, engraving and repairing shoes.

There had been a well-known singer around Warrnambool known as Rocking Ricky Randall who'd fronted a popular local band called The Ghost Riders. After he died a tribute night was held for him at the Palais Theatre in Warrnambool and I was asked if I would sing. I actually took a bit of convincing to do the night as I had decided to give up on pipedreams and settle for a normal life. As I've said, I had never treated singing as just a hobby. So whenever I was exposed to it, I felt the same insistent, burning passion welling up inside of me.

Maybe it can be compared to smoking. Some people can smoke socially and never develop a habit, whereas others just need one taste and it becomes an addiction. I was like that with singing. I couldn't just do it casually. Every time I performed I was overcome with a desire to make it my life. It seemed to consume me, as if I were awakening a force within myself. To continue the analogy, some addictions can kill you. My brief experience with Barry Shields, the sax player, had taught me that music, or the relentless pursuit of a dream, can lead to a nightmare that inevitably ends in death.

So it was with some trepidation that I agreed to perform. The Palais was packed that night. Over two thousand people had turned up to pay their respects to a well-known and well-loved singer, which only increased the pressure on us to make sure the night was an appropriate tribute.

A lot of the local musicians had come together for this night, and what I had agreed to under pressure became a truly memorable occasion for me. It was great to be back on the stage, great to let that part of me come alive again. We sang a lot of the old favourites and then, at the end of the night, it was time for me—the real me—to take centre stage.

I was quite well known for my rock and roll and felt

confident on stage, giving the audience what they expected. As the end of the night drew near a eulogy was read for the dead rocker. Then the musicians and everyone else fell silent and it was just me, standing in the spotlight.

Now it was time for me to really sing, to give the audience a part of my soul, to expose who I really was. Suddenly, for the first time in years I felt real fear as I prepared to sing. Murmurs from the audience began to interrupt the silence and people looked as though they were wondering what was going to happen. My mouth felt dry as I swallowed and then, as always seems to happen, something deep within me took over. I stood on that stage in front of all of those people and sang that wonderful song that is the closest popular music can get to an aria, 'Amazing Grace'.

As the last word echoed through the Palais, it was me again, coming back to my real self, standing proudly in the centre of the stage. No longer lost in the song, I looked out at a sea of faces staring up at me. I swear some people actually had their mouths open. Then it happened, the cheering. And it was unlike anything I'd heard before. It seemed the whole audience, all two thousand of them, was moving as one towards the stage. I actually felt a little fearful as they surged forward, cheering and yelling, wanting more of the music, wanting to share and taste something of the passion that filled my soul.

That was the first time I had performed anything like the music I loved to an audience since those teenage days at the Shepparton Italian barbecue. The reaction I got that night has never left me. Perhaps the fact that I was known as a rocker surprised people and they were a bit shocked to hear the sound that came from me. But I knew after that night that I couldn't keep denying, to myself or to anyone else, who I was. Classical singing was as much a part of me as my passion for my family. To resist or deny it was to live half a life, to be half the person you can be.

Reality always hits home, of course, and as much as I would have loved to keep performing classics, there really wasn't much call for it in Warrnambool. Then, not long after the tribute night, there was a knock on our door. It was a couple of guys asking me to join their band; they had a regular gig at the Mid-City Hotel in town. They convinced me to go along and listen to them.

I walked in that first night determined I would just look and listen. But I was in for a big surprise. I'd never seen a set-up quite like what I saw on stage. The band played dinner music, soft melodic tunes, while people ate. Then, as the night wore on, the members of the band all swapped instruments and the rock and roll would start.

During a break in the music I was introduced to all the band members, who asked me to sit on the side of the stage. The drummer's name was Gary, and he looked over at me. 'Do you know this one?' he whispered. It was Peter Allen's 'I Still Call Australia Home', and I didn't need much convincing to get up on stage and sing it.

The bug had me and I agreed to work out twenty-five songs with the band so that I could help them out over the Christmas period. We did songs like 'Blue Moon', along with ballads by the likes of Roy Orbison and The Platters.

I ended up spending eight fairly crazy years working at the Mid-City, with the band changing members and direction along the way. We soon built up a bit of a cult following and there were nights when we had that place really thumping. People were hanging out the doors, so the owner added a big function room. We went through the ballads and did cabaret-type performances for those in the dining room and, instead of having a break between sets, we'd go straight to the function room for some rock and roll before returning to the dining room and doing ballads again.

Not long after we started at the Mid-City, Mister Minit closed its shop in Warrnambool. Sharon and I were not doing too well financially since the money I made from the band was not enough to support our family. We had grown to four by this time with the birth of our daughter Cathy in March 1984, so we decided to move out of Warrnambool altogether and try our luck somewhere else.

Sharon and I went through some pretty rough times in the early years. When we first moved out of Warrnambool we lived at the back of a milkbar owned by some friends of Sharon's in Doveton, near Dandenong. I didn't know anything about Melbourne or the suburbs, but the name Doveton sounded nice and I thought it would be a pretty place to live in.

I was soon to learn that just as you can't judge a person before you've met them, suburbs are not to be judged by their names. I have nothing against the people who live in Doveton, but it was not made up of tree-lined lanes with doves flying overhead as I'd imagined. The shop where we stayed was built entirely of concrete, so it was a bit like living in a crypt. It was also cold and depressing, so as soon as we could we rented a house in a suburb called Keysborough. I got a job at Mister Minit at the Bayside Shopping Centre in Frankston and life settled into something of a routine.

I was still doing gigs at the Mid-City, so for many years

it was a pretty weird time. I would work during the day and when I knocked off I'd have to drive the four hours to Warrnambool, perform for four or five hours and then drive home again. After a few hours sleep it would be time for me to go to work again. Some weeks we would be booked for three nights—Thursday, Friday and Saturday—so I would make the trip up and down on the Thursday and Friday nights, and stay in one of the motel rooms on the Saturday night.

There were also the nights, particularly during winter, when it seemed we were entertaining ourselves more than the audience. Bands can attract quite unique characters and over the years I was fortunate to share the stage with some really great and unusual people. Some nights we would deliberately sing the wrong words to songs, just to see if anyone was listening. Other times we would give each other stupid dares just to keep the energy levels up, especially on those quiet winter nights when only a few people ventured out of their homes. I can still clearly remember one particularly dead night when one of the band members actually started to nod off during a song.

Disputes between band members also were fairly commonplace and sometimes fights would break out in the middle of a gig. There was one musician in Warrnambool who was known to be a real sook. If he cracked it during a set he would unplug his guitar and go home, leaving the band standing there in front of the audience with no guitar player. I had heard of his reputation but didn't quite believe it as the band scene can be a bit gossipy at times. Then I played with him for a while and learned that every word was true.

And so it was for many years, nights of singing and the

constant travelling. Some nights I swear I don't know how I got home in one piece—what with the absolute exhaustion that came over me as the car travelled the familiar road back and forth between Warrnambool and Keysborough. But I always felt this need to get home, to be with my family when I woke up.

The exhaustion became even worse on the nights we worked the two rooms, largely because the singing and the performing was so different in the two venues. It meant that, within seconds of moving from one to the other, I had to switch from sweet ballads and songs by Roy Orbison and Elvis to screaming my lungs out to a rock crowd. By this time I was smoking up to sixty cigarettes a day and had to keep my throat smooth, so I thought, by drinking whisky and brandy throughout the night. I don't think I ever got drunk as we worked so hard I probably sweated out everything I took in. But I also drank gallons of strong coffee just to keep myself going for the trip home.

Sometimes it seemed that someone must be watching over me, keeping me safe, because in the hundreds of kilometres I drove each week nothing bad ever really happened. The law of averages said I should have had an accident but, take it or leave it, I really felt there was something guiding me because the more tired I became while driving, the slower the car would travel. Sometimes I would turn off to the side of the road and sleep. And whenever that happened I'd wake up and, just for a second, I felt I was a child again, sleeping with the family on the side of the road.

Looking back, I suppose it would have been a lot easier to have worked nine to five and led a normal life. But that was never an option. Singing was an integral part of who I was. If there were times when I questioned the sanity of my lifestyle, there were also times when I knew why I was doing it, why I drove myself (literally and figuratively) to such lengths to perform. I felt wanted and needed up there on the stage, it was affirmation for me that I could do something really well.

The very slow nights when only a few people dropped in for dinner or a drink gave us a chance to relax a little, as we'd only play one room and be able to interact with the audience. One night I noticed a woman sitting alone at a table with a drink, eyes closed, as we did a set of Roy Orbison numbers. I don't know what it was about her and perhaps it was simply that she was different from the usual crowd who came to see us. She was middle aged, but she hadn't bothered to do herself up for a big night out. She seemed quite content to sit and listen as we did the set. Then she got up and left. The next week it was the same. As soon as we finished the Roy Orbison set, she finished her drink and left.

I was intrigued. I wanted to know what it was that brought this woman here week after week. I could sense that she was here for the music, that she was moved to a different place and time by what she heard. The next week, before she had a chance to leave, I walked over to her table and asked if I could join her.

We chatted for a while before I asked what I needed to know. 'I hope you don't mind me asking, but why is it that you always leave at the same time every night?'

She looked at me and I noticed a tear in her eye as she spoke. 'I just love Roy Orbison. You give me the chance to sit here and listen to him sing. I can shut my eyes and believe that it is him in the room, singing to me.'

There is perhaps no greater compliment for a singer than to be told he sounds like Roy Orbison. For me it was confirmation that all those hours of sitting alone, of practising for years, trying to master every inflection and nuance of his voice, had been worthwhile. As I sat with this woman I felt genuinely touched that I had been able to move her so emotionally with my voice.

She told me she had been a fan of his for years, and we became like kindred spirits as she shared with me her wonderful memories of that remarkable man. Then she invited me to her place where, she said, she wanted to share with me some of her most treasured possessions.

She and her husband lived at the back of a milkbar in Warrnambool, and the next time I stayed overnight I went to visit them. They were a really terrific couple. She took me out the back and there she opened a box. Inside were photographs she had taken of herself and Roy Orbison when he visited Warrnambool for the last time in his life. She told me he had been a very gracious and lovely man and had spent about half an hour chatting to her at the airport before he left.

I felt honoured to be sharing such special memories with this woman. I suppose all singers have their own particular idol, someone who is held up as the ultimate at their craft. For me, it was of course Mario Lanza, but Roy Orbison is not far behind. And to most singers he is of course The One, the singer's singer.

Meeting that special lady and sharing her memories brought home to me yet again that singing and music has the power to emotionally transform a person, and I felt so privileged to be blessed with the ability to have an impact on someone's life, no matter how small. Among my most treasured possessions today are copies of those photographs, which were given to me on the condition that they never be published or given away. So they sit in my own shoebox treasure chest, a memento of the spirit that to me, is part of what music is all about.

I have also witnessed the damage that music can do. There is a strange allure to the lights of the stage. For years I had watched as women making meaningless declarations of love gave themselves freely to musicians, hoping that a little of the magic would stay with them after the groping and groaning in the back of the car was over. Not every band member was like that, of course, but there were always one or two willing to take advantage of lonely souls.

I often thought of Barry Shields, the sax player, and the many others like him who must have believed the empty promises and tried to make reality as good as their time on stage. And all of it is because I know that no matter how good a performer you are, the image people see on stage is just that, an image. No one can live their life with so much promise and excitement, and real life is the same for performers as it is for anyone else. The lights and the music and the adoration of the audience might seem like a dream come true for some. But for me at the end of the night it was hoping my old car would get me home, worrying about paying the bills and getting up for my 'real' job the next day.

There were also the times when the dream would be tantalisingly close. Often when big name acts came to town they would stay at the Mid-City. So for a brief time I would be allowed into that zone again, sharing drinks with the stars from Hot Chocolate, or other well-known singers of the day.

Sometimes the function room would be booked by other bands for the night, so we'd perform in the dining room while they played. One night the bass player in our band whispered to me on stage, 'Look who's watching us play.' I turned towards the back of the room and saw some of the guys from the band playing the function room, the Mick Hamilton Trio. Mick Hamilton had been with a well-known Australian band in the sixties called the Vibrants. Also in the band was a guy called Gary Young, who had been the drummer with Daddy Cool. I was star-struck, of course, and went in the other room to meet them. They asked me to join them for a drink after the gig. I stayed with them until about five o'clock in the morning, singing and chatting about music.

Their band had a regular gig at the Beehive in Melbourne, and they asked me to come along one night. I went to see them and couldn't believe it when I was introduced to the crowd as a guest singer. I stood on that stage and did a few of the old favourites, then Gary asked me if I would do 'Crying'. I should explain that to do proper justice to a Roy Orbison song a singer has to prepare himself. I had just been doing rock stuff and wasn't really ready to launch into 'Crying'.

'Go on,' said Gary. It was one of the songs we had done together after the gig at the Mid-City.

'Okay.' I smiled at him. 'I'll do "Crying" if you'll do "Eagle Rock".'

Mick Hamilton looked at me and said, 'Not a chance. He won't do it.'

I'm not sure of all the ins and outs of what had happened, but I guessed that there must have been some bad water under the bridge since the old Daddy Cool days. But 'Eagle Rock' is one of those songs instantly recognised by millions of Australians as something of an anthem to the early seventies.

I looked across at Gary and said, 'Well, sorry mate, that's the deal.'

The next thing I knew the familiar starting notes filled the room. The crowd went crazy and I looked across at Mick who had a look of utter disbelief on his face. Of course I kept my part of the deal and sang 'Crying'.

I kept in touch with those guys for quite a while until other things in my life took over. When I did try to contact them again, the phone numbers had changed and so I gave up.

Another time the singer Frank Ifield was performing in Warrnambool and was staying at the Mid-City. I asked the receptionist if she would pass on to him that I would very much like to meet him. She looked at me as if she'd been asked the same thing a thousand times that night. 'How many people do you think would want to meet him?' she asked. She might as well have said, 'Who do you think you are?' But I absolutely loved Frank Ifield and I wasn't going to be deterred.

'Please,' I asked, 'Just let him know that I'd love to meet him tomorrow morning before he leaves.'

I sat in reception the next morning waiting and waiting, hoping that even if she hadn't passed on the message I might just get to see one of my idols in the flesh. A man came and paid a hotel bill, my heart leapt, thinking it was Frank Ifield.

But it wasn't and I felt really dejected. Obviously, even if he'd got the message, Ifield just wanted to be left alone. I got up and went to the toilet. As I came out I noticed a figure standing in the corner of the reception area wearing a hat and coat. He looked across at me and said, 'Peter?' It was him, it was Frank Ifield! The receptionist had done what I asked and he had gone out of his way to meet me. It was sheer luck that I was still there, since I'd all but given up and was about to head home.

He was really friendly and we chatted about music and what I was doing. I told him I had been to his show the night before and how much I admired his voice. He then asked me whether I could give his driver directions to Ballarat. I stood out in the car park that morning leaning on the bonnet of his car and felt like a king. Before he left he shook my hand and said, 'Never give up. It's a very hard road, but if you've got the heart for it, if it's truly what you want, it will happen.'

As his car drove off, I felt elated but at the same time sad. I might have shared a brief moment with a true star, but here I was, standing in the car park as he drove off to the next destination. I could show him where he should go on the map, but who would ever show me which road to take?

The worst time of the year in Warrnambool was when the May races were on. It is a huge event for the town, but we were booked to do gigs most nights of the week. So I'd work in Melbourne on the Monday and Tuesday, then drive to Warrnambool on Tuesday night. I'd sing for four or five hours, drive home, have a quick nap and a shower and go to work in Melbourne. Then I'd do it again on Wednesday and

Thursday nights. I usually worked late in the shop on a Friday night, so I could have a snooze on Saturday before heading off to Warrnambool again for the Saturday night.

Most years during the racing carnival Sharon would drive me up and back, so that I could catch a bit of sleep in the car. But one year she was heavily pregnant with our third daughter, Lisa, so I was travelling up and down all week alone. The band did the two rooms most nights, so there was no break in between sets. Also, the race crowd wanted to party, so we were called on to do encores which made the night even later than usual.

I remember that year, 1988, really well since not only was Sharon pregnant but I woke up on a Monday morning with laryngitis. I was still able to sing as the mechanism for talking and singing is quite different, but I felt dreadful and the week passed in a blur of alcohol, coffee and throat medication. I shudder now when I think of the abuse I put my voice through, not to mention the distances I managed to travel without hurting myself or anyone else.

While I certainly wouldn't recommend that anyone put themselves through that sort of regime, I sometimes think that the strength of my voice today has a lot to do with the days in the band. Not only was I using my voice for hours at a time, I was singing songs with such variety that I had to develop notes and tones covering a huge range. My years of mimicking artists meant I developed a range that allowed me to sing the very high notes and then change to the very low. At other times I think my voice is still strong *in spite* of the years of gruelling punishment it took. Many of the nights we spent performing for hours at a time have blurred and it is difficult to separate one night from another.

But there came a time when the smoking, drinking and screaming my lungs out took its toll.

It must have been in the middle of the night. I was singing about the third encore of Roy Orbison's 'Crying' when the taste of whisky and smokes was replaced by a strange metallic sensation in my mouth. I wiped the sweat from my chin, and when I looked at my hand, I saw blood. I was bleeding from the throat. I think I went into emotional autopilot as I drove myself home and told Sharon what had happened who booked me a doctor's appointment.

Waiting is the worst part of medical trials, and at each stage—from the GP to the specialist and back to the GP—I kept telling myself I was worried about nothing. They would tell me it was all okay and it was just a minor glitch. But somehow, I knew deep down something bad must have happened, that my throat could no longer cope with the abuse I had put it through.

When the specialist told me I needed an operation to remove nodules from my throat, my immediate reaction was one of relief. It was fixable, they could operate and put me right again. Then came the words that spiralled me down to the lowest depths of hopelessness.

'I'm afraid you'll never sing again,' the surgeon said.

As he spoke the helplessness washed over me and I knew I was at the mercy of some force bigger than myself. I saw myself as a child trapped in a car with a monster, as a teenager standing thirty metres above the ground while a machine chewed my arm off. I was locked in a lonely hotel room in the middle of nowhere, grieving for the wife who had left me and the baby who had been taken from me.

Now the one thing that had sustained me through all the

ups and downs of my life was also being taken away. And what hurt most was that I knew it had been all my fault.

I had been given a gift, a talent to sing. But through years of abuse and misuse it was gone. Screaming my lungs out night after night, smoking, drinking, living on little or no sleep, had taken its toll. I detested bullying and violence and yet because of me, my voice, my passion, had been bullied and buffeted until, taken for granted for so long, it had said that it had had enough.

It could give no more.

*You'll never sing again.*

## CHAPTER 11

## I WAS A MARRIED MAN WITH THREE CHILDREN

and I really didn't have the time to be wallowing in self-pity. I had faced—and overcome—much else in my life. Even though I felt as though my heart had been ripped from my chest, I got on with things the best I could.

Perhaps in some ways it was almost a relief. If I could no longer sing, maybe the burning ambition that had guided so much of my life would die; I would at last be free of the incessant urge to sing, to make it my life.

I had to constantly remind myself that I was a very lucky man. The problem wasn't going to kill me, I had a lovely family, I was young and, as I had found in the past, things could always get worse than you imagined. Of course, the internal dialogue I had with myself was just empty words. My singing was so much a part of who I was that I felt like half a person, but I picked up the pieces and prepared to live without music.

Sharon's mum, Anita, had started a relationship with a terrific man called Victor. He was involved with selling cookware, and it took very little to convince me to leave Mister Minit and try my hand at door-to-door selling. For the next few years my life became almost normal as I worked hard at trying to make ends meet. When the selling would peter out I would get a job again at Mister Minit, then I would leave again and try my hand at selling.

There is a saying in sales that the hardest door to open is your own. I suppose what that means is that in order to do well, you really have to be motivated. It wasn't that I didn't believe in the product I was selling, and when I put my mind to it I was quite good, but the enthusiasm didn't come easily. And the harsh reality of selling is that if you don't sell you don't get paid.

There were times when things were pretty tight financially and we really struggled. But the kids always had a roof over their heads and food in their bellies, and they always knew they were loved. Yes, it's an old cliché, but love *is* free, and we were at least able to give the girls plenty of that.

But, as the song says, love don't pay the rent. And one day in particular sums up how bad things were at times, and yet how your fortune can change when you have very little to begin with. I had enough money to put petrol in the car, so I decided to follow up a lead on a sale in Korumburra. I had a five-dollar note and some coins in my pocket. Before setting off, I gave the five dollars to Sharon and asked her to go to the TAB and put a bet on a horse. Neither I nor my family were heavy gamblers, but we followed the races and I'd developed a working man's knowledge of the track. I don't know why, but I had a good feeling about this particular horse. And it was only five dollars, which wasn't enough to pay the rent, so it seemed okay to try our luck.

I drove all the way to my appointment only to find the people weren't home, so I'd travelled over a hundred and twenty kilometres, wasted a day and used all that petrol for nothing. The whole bloody day had turned into a shambles and I was convinced it was only going to get worse. Cursing the people I was meant to see, the whole world and me in particular, I put my hand in my pocket to see how much I had in change. It was exactly one dollar and twenty cents, not even enough for a sandwich, let alone a meal. With the money in my hand, I went to the nearest shop and asked for half a cup of coffee.

The shopkeeper must have taken pity on me since he gave me a full cup. But as I got back into my car, I spilt the boiling drink all over myself. As hot and painful as it was, though, I didn't yell out. I simply sat there with the liquid burning into my skin and, as much as I tried not to, I began to cry. The pain of the coffee meant nothing in itself, it just brought to a head the fact that I could no longer cope with all the heartbreak and anguish that had been festering for days.

Why is it, I'd often asked myself, that those who work hardest seem to end up with so much less? I'd worked since I was fourteen—hard, physical and, at times, dangerous work—yet I couldn't even afford to buy myself a proper cup of coffee.

I sat there sinking deeper and deeper into self-pity when there was a tapping on the car door. I wound the window down and looked at the woman who stood there.

'Is everything all right?' she asked. She looked genuinely concerned, and so I told her that I was having a bad day, a client had cancelled and I had no money.

She looked down at me and, whether out of pity or genuine concern, she said, 'Why don't you come back to my place? I need to replace some of my cookware, and I know my sister would be interested in buying some.'

I felt like a rescued puppy as I followed her to her home, where she rang her sister and told her that the cookware man was there. Her sister brought several friends with her. After I'd straightened myself out, I did a demonstration of how to use the stuff and ended up with orders for five sets.

I really don't know what would have happened had that lovely woman not come along. I returned home that day with money in my pocket, the deposits the people had paid me, and instead of hating the world I had a real spring in my step.

'Sharon!' I yelled as I walked through the door, 'you'll never guess what happened today.'

Sharon was smiling as she walked into the kitchen. 'Well, I'll bet *you'll* never guess what happened,' she laughed. Then it was a race to see who could get their good news out first. Sharon won. 'That horse,' she said with a huge grin right across her face, half from excitement and half at the puzzled look on my face. 'You know something, it won! And it paid nine hundred and eighty-nine dollars.'

I'd completely forgotten about the bet. And on seeing that look in her eyes, I grabbed her and we leapt around the kitchen like kids at Christmas.

Yes, it was one of those days. And it summed up just how we lived . . . swinging from real hardship, not knowing where the next dollar was coming from, to fabulous, unimaginable happiness when everything went right.

I alternated between the shoe repairs and selling cookware for a few years. Sometimes I would do both, working in the shop during the day and selling at night, so at times I was bringing in good money and things were going well.

We moved back to Warrnambool for a short while and I set up in business selling cookware in the local area. One of the first people I employed was Dad, who was actually a really good salesman. He was good with people and they genuinely liked him and trusted what he was telling them. Then the sales seemed to dry up and we moved again, hoping our luck would change.

We finally moved to Dandenong and took over a place the kids came to call the 'ghost house'. It was quite confronting from the outside, with big steel gates protecting the old red brick house from intruders. From the moment we moved in strange things happened. Tiles often fell off the bathroom wall, but only as someone was settling into the bath, never during the day when no one was around. Doors refused to shut, almost as if some invisible hand was holding onto them or a foot was preventing them from closing properly. Mould grew in the rooms for no reason, and we seemed to have a constant stream of maintenance men in to fix problems for which no cause could be found.

The creaks and groans that are part of a normal house became more ominous, especially at night when the kids were convinced someone was walking through their rooms.

Sharon and I told them it was the wind, the house settling or possums in the roof. But we too even as adults, found things a bit too weird in that house. One night we got a babysitter for the girls while we went out. When we came home we were shocked to find her sitting upright in her chair, looking pale and fearful. As she walked to the door she told us, 'I don't know what it is about this house and I'm sorry, but I'm never coming back here to babysit.'

The atmosphere in the house became so bad that no one would stay, not even our own relatives. Everyone sensed there was something wrong and, even if they'd travelled a long way to visit, they refused to stay overnight. Eventually, we contacted the owner of the house. She was an elderly Italian woman, and she arrived at the house one day and reassured us she would sort out the problem. Sharon and I watched as she marched down the hallway into the master bedroom. After some muffled noises, she emerged smiling. 'My husband died in this house. He never liked visitors', she said. I have no idea what happened in that room, but the problems stopped after her visit.

Some of the many places we stayed in over the years became home for a while, others were just stopovers while we waited to go somewhere else. I never really had a sense of place, of belonging. Perhaps it was a hangover from my childhood, of always knowing I should not get too attached to a place as we would soon be on the move again. Whatever it was, it made for an uneasy sense of restlessness that I had no control over. As much as I hated it, I felt that no matter where I was or who I was with, it seemed that spiritually I was drifting.

Even today I wonder how my not being able to sing affected what I had become. My life wasn't that bad, but I always had this unrelenting feeling that something was missing, I wasn't being the person I knew I could be. I was actually very good at my job and had no trouble getting work at various shoe-repair shops around the suburbs. And I must have had a fairly good reputation because one day a man who owned a little shoe-repair place in Hawthorn approached me. He was going overseas for several years and needed someone to take over while he was away. He'd actually had someone in already, but things hadn't worked out and the business was now very rundown.

This was my chance to make something of my life, so I negotiated with him and took the shop over on vendor terms. It was a tiny little place, really only half a shop, but had been there for years. Some of the equipment was nearly a hundred years old and it was impossible not to feel the presence of those who had come before me and taken so much pride in their work. In some strange way, I felt a kind of responsibility to them, and became determined to make a go of it, not just for my sake but also so that the shop might rekindle the popularity and success it obviously once had.

I have always found working with my hands very satisfying and I took an enormous amount of pride in the work I did in that little shop. But, with time to think, I also became increasingly aware that things were not going too well at home. My marriage was faltering.

Sharon and I were very young when we married. I think at the time I was looking for a place and a person to feel safe with, someone I could love and, in doing so, get over the disaster of my first marriage. But, as the years passed, we found ourselves arguing and bickering about small issues, things that really weren't that important.

We tried hard to keep the marriage going, if only for the sake of the girls. We went to counselling and I left home a few times, so that both of us could try to find some peace. Then I'd miss Sharon and the kids so badly I'd move back. But we both finally realised it would be better for the girls if we weren't together. The constant niggling and fighting was no way to bring up children and towards the end the girls' grades at school had begun to suffer. We both knew it was time to make the break and be honest for the sake of everyone.

I can never speak badly of Sharon and I know that many people find it hard to understand our relationship. We grew up together and we have raised a beautiful family that I am so proud of. When I finally moved out of the house she would bring my dinner to the caravan park I was staying at; we actually supported each other through the end of our marriage.

There has never been an issue with custody or access to the kids; we have always made any decisions regarding the girls' futures together. We still celebrate family occasions such as birthdays, and today Sharon remains one of my best friends and confidantes.

Ending our marriage was one of the hardest things either of us has had to do. I don't know that I would have coped with the breakdown if we hadn't supported each other. But for both of us, leaving behind a marriage that had died years before meant that we could start again, both with our friendship and the rest of our lives.

Once the break was made, we both reassessed what we were doing and the direction our lives were taking. Sharon decided to go back to school, and she now teaches remedial reading and works as an integration aide in schools.

For me the road to the future was a lot less certain. Along the way I have fallen into many potholes, some so big I never thought I would climb out of them.

## CHAPTER 12

### IT WAS A STRANGE FEELING BEING SINGLE.

I had never really been alone before; even after the break-up of my first marriage I'd had Sally to care for. The three girls stayed with Sharon, so now it was just me. I moved around a bit before settling for a time in a flat near the shop in Hawthorn. Life became a little more structured and my mind turned to singing once again. I hadn't really allowed myself to think about it for a few years. It was something I'd had to forget about. It was gone. But that hadn't stopped the yearning, the wishing that somehow my voice might return.

I started the first tentative steps, testing my voice when I was alone in the shop or the flat, singing a few bars, softly at first, and waiting to feel the telltale signs of strain. Somehow, it didn't happen. For some unfathomable reason, I found I could make those notes and sing free of pain. If anything, and much to my surprise and joy, my voice was even stronger than it had been before the operation.

I'd sing and it all came out just fine, so fine that I found it impossible to stop the excitement and the hope that bubbled around in my head and made my throat dry whenever I prepared to start. It was like diving off a cliff, frightening at first but then as smooth, as wonderful and as free as a caress.

The only way I can explain the feeling is by relating it to the time I thought my arm had been chopped off, and the relief I felt when I found it was still there. I began to think that perhaps doctors always give the worst-case scenario, just in case things don't work out. I had been told as a teenager that I would never use my arm again, and yet I went on to become a black belt in karate.

Each time I practised singing, my confidence grew. And for the life of me I couldn't get out of my mind the little lizards—skinks I think they're called—we would catch as kids. If you grabbed them by the tail, the tail would come off between your fingers while the lizards ran away. But after a while a new tail always grows back, stronger and tougher than before. Could this be what was happening to me? My voice had been taken from me, but now it was back, stronger than before.

Maybe it was the fact that I had rested my voice for a few years, or maybe it was some sort of miracle. I didn't want to question it too much. So few things happen in life that can truly be called luck that, superstitiously I thought to question too deeply might jeopardise my good fortune.

About six months after the breakdown of my marriage, I began a relationship with a woman I will call Carol, who worked in a shop nearby. We had been friends for a while, as she often called into the shop and sometimes we would share a coffee or lunch. She would regularly bring me chocolates, teasing me that I needed to be sweeter.

Our relationship was to last for nearly four years, one of the most romantic and emotional periods of my life. I have not a moment's regret about the time I spent with that beautiful, passionate woman. Carol taught me so much about life and about myself. She made me be the best person I could be. She saw beyond the cobbler's uniform of flannelette shirt, shorts and workboots. I had always wanted to get my ear pierced, so we went together to the chemist where she held my hand through the pain. We shopped for clothes, and she took me to the hairdresser. For the first time in my life I felt a sense of pride in myself as I walked down the street with this beautiful woman on my arm.

What Carol taught me, however, was much more than just how to make surface changes. My voice had become strong enough that I started to sing with the band again, although the enjoyment I'd always had from it was beginning to wane. It was difficult to describe now how I felt about singing. I'd had success on a provincial level, and to many people that should be enough. But now that my voice was back it was the classical songs I dreamt of again, with a burning passion.

Logically any chance I had of making it as a singer had passed me by. I was now an old rocker in my late thirties, reliving and performing memories of times gone by. But Carol's insight was able to detect the underlying passion, even though it was so deep it was almost buried.

I had reverted to my childhood habit of only allowing myself the luxury of singing classically when I was in the comfort and privacy of the bathroom, along with the suds and the steam.

One morning I came out of the bathroom and found myself face to face with Carol. She was staring at me and, though I couldn't work out what she was thinking, I was sure she was angry about something.

'You didn't tell me you could sing,' she said, as if accusing me of hiding something.

'Aw, c'mon,' I replied, smiling broadly as I walked to the kitchen and poured myself a cup of coffee. 'You've been to the gigs. You've heard me sing.'

'No, you bastard,' she retorted. 'I mean *really* sing. You didn't tell me you could really sing.'

She stared even harder at me and I was a little unnerved by her intensity. Perhaps she realised she had touched a nerve because she relaxed as she took my hand and spoke gently.

'I worked in the wardrobe department of the West Australian State Opera for ten years,' she said. 'I've never heard a voice like yours. You've got to do something with it. It's a gift.'

From that morning, Carol embarked on a mission. It was as if she could see into my soul and had suddenly recognised the person I had always wanted to be. What had always been my secret dream was now shared with someone else. And the sharing made it seem that much more real. Someone at last believed in me as a classical singer. Having someone to lean on, to give joy to, made it seem just that little bit possible that this dream of mine might not be so hollow after all. Maybe it could become very real.

The first positive step I took was to look up the names of singing teachers in the phone book. Even then, it was a while before I took the plunge and actually made an appointment with one of them.

I drove myself to Stephen Grant's house in North Fitzroy, knowing that he would laugh at me, tell me to go back to cobbling and forget about singing. I had the feeling he thought he was wasting his time when he questioned me on the phone. I had been honest and told him that I was nearly forty, had no formal training and smoked sixty cigarettes a day. (I also told him I was fat and bald. I wanted him to be pleasantly surprised about one thing at least.)

I was horribly nervous as I walked up the path to Stephen's house. His wife was doing some gardening, and smiled encouragingly at me. I knocked on the door and took a deep breath, suddenly acutely aware of the stench of cigarettes that followed me everywhere.

When Stephen opened the door, he was pretty much what I expected from our phone conversation, a slight man with a soft Canadian accent. I shook his offered hand and stepped into his music room. I had never felt like such a phony in my life. It was one thing to be told I sounded good in the shower, it was quite another to actually sing for someone who knew what they were talking about and what they were listening to.

We exchanged a few pleasantries, and I reaffirmed all the drawbacks we had gone through on the phone. No education, heavy smoker—and not a clue about opera. He obviously didn't want to waste my time or his, so without much chit-chat he asked me to sing. I was so scared, certain that my dreams were about to be shattered by this quiet man. But I shut my eyes and I was back in the caravan park, hearing for the first time the voice of Mario Lanza coming from the gramophone. Only this time the voice was coming from me.

A few bars into 'Serenade', I allowed myself to open my eyes just a little, half expecting to see Stephen checking his watch or staring out the window. But he was staring straight at me, his eyes so wide that I felt for a moment I must be naked. I stopped singing, but he gestured for me to go on. I finished the song and stood waiting for the verdict that could change my life.

Almost as though speaking to himself, Stephen muttered, 'Amazing . . . extraordinary . . . rare.' He paused after each word, allowing them to sink in, to hang in the air for a moment. I swear I could feel a fluttering in my heart and I know my head was spinning. But it was beginning to sink in. He liked me—he really thought I could sing!

I still couldn't believe it, so I had to reassure myself. 'You're not just saying that because you want the money?' I said. I cringe now when I think that I actually asked him that. What I was doing, in my painfully ignorant way, was reassuring myself that what I was hearing was true, certainly not meaning to offend or question Stephen's ethics. I must have sounded like a complete prick. And I shall be forever grateful that he didn't kick me out there and then.

At that moment, what had been my lifelong ambition had become a tangible possibility. I knew that the commitment had to come from me as well as those around me. From then on, my determination led, among other things, to finally making a real attempt to give up smoking. I knew in my heart that if I was to have any chance of making it I had to give up that habit of a lifetime. Not only that, but lessons with Stephen were not cheap and something had to go if I was to afford them.

I was to learn that Stephen is a man of few words. When he does speak it is with deliberation and thought. A few weeks after I started, I was walking through their garden when his wife, Francesca, motioned for me to join her.

'You know, Stephen will probably never tell you this, but after you left on that first day, he told me that he had just heard a voice in a million. "Phenomenal" and "sensational" were the words he used to describe your voice.' She smiled at me as she continued. 'I've never heard him use those words about anyone before.'

Francesca went back to her garden and I walked into my lesson almost in a trance. All of those years of dreaming and longing, finally accepting that it was out of my reach, just a pipedream, and now it was becoming real.

Stephen was—is—a wonderful teacher. He was patient and calm, and never made me feel stupid or uneducated. I'm sure there were times when he must have been incredulous at my lack of musical knowledge, but he led me gently through, building on my strengths while working on my weaknesses. There were times when I couldn't afford to pay him, so he would give me an old pair of shoes to mend. I suspect he sometimes deliberately ruined shoes just so that I could keep going to him.

Although I was now learning the finer points of opera, I still had no real idea of how to progress to the next level. I saw an advertisement for a performance of *La Bohème* that was being put on by the Eastern Metropolitan Opera Company. I decided to try my luck, and went to the company to tell them that I was a tenor, and interested in joining their company. The response I got was under-whelming, to say the least. I suppose they have many people approach them who think they have a voice, and a man of my age with no experience probably wasn't what they were looking for. I ended up buying a ticket to the performance; it was to be my first taste of what real opera was like. For nearly my whole life, I had been consumed by the music written in distant lands for audiences long ago. Now, on a rainy night in Melbourne, I was finally to experience that joy for myself.

I sat in the audience that night, and felt like a kid again. Watching the performance, something inside me came alive. As the arias filled the auditorium, I felt the breath knocked out of me. The beauty and the passion of words written to move an audience, the human drama being played out in front of me—it was one of the most emotional experiences of my life. I didn't realise I was holding my breath until an aria ended and I allowed myself to breathe again, holding my hand against a heart that felt it was about to burst.

When it was time for the tenors to take the stage, I leaned forward, waiting to be moved, hoping I wouldn't cry. But my heart dropped. The intensity, the passion of the drama was missing. I was familiar with the songs as I had studied some of them with Stephen, and I knew what each nuance and inflection was meant to convey. But it wasn't there.

I walked outside at interval feeling slightly flattened. I had carried the music within me for so much of my life that I think I felt slightly protective of it. I was uneducated and only just learning about the origins and meaning of the words, but I'd always had an instinctive love of the music. To see it performed with scant regard for its beauty upset me at a level I couldn't quite comprehend.

I was lost in thought when I felt a tap on my arm. Wrapped in a huge raincoat stood a little woman who I recognised as sitting next to me during the performance. She stared up at me as if we were old friends.

'You're a tenor, aren't you?' she asked.

I was taken aback, and asked how she could possibly know. She gently touched my arm again and smiled. 'There's something inside you,' she said. 'I could see it in your eyes as you were watching the opera. You wear your heart on your sleeve.'

We chatted for a while and I told her where I was working and my dreams of singing opera. Just before it was time to go back inside she said, 'You should always listen to your heart and follow your dream.'

I didn't think any more about that meeting until a few weeks later, when I heard the shop door open. I had been out the back singing and as I walked into the shop I saw a raincoat with a little lady wrapped inside it. It was the woman from the night of the opera.

'Hello, do you remember me?'

'The night of *La Bohème*, yes I do remember.'

She looked around the tiny shop before asking, 'What record was that you just had playing?'

I was slightly embarrassed as I answered her question. 'That wasn't a record playing. I was singing.'

'Well then, I'm so glad I came to see you.' She looked up at me with a tear in her eye and a stunned expression on her face. The next words she said affected me deeply. 'I was

right. There is something special about you. What a magnificent voice.'

So it was that for a brief time my customers became my
audience. They would listen as I sang while I mended shoes,
obviously moved by my voice. I tried to find contentment
in the knowledge that at least I had an avenue of expression,
that even in my own small way I was reaching out to others
with my music.

It wasn't long after this that another woman came into
my shop while I was singing out the back. I walked to the
counter and was only too happy to oblige when she asked
me to sing for her.

Then she reached into her handbag and took out a piece
of paper. 'I think that you should ring this telephone
number and speak to this man. His name is David Kram and
he might be able to help you.'

Before I had time to ask her anything else, she wished
me luck and left. I stood there with the piece of paper in my
hand, not sure if I'd just dealt with a madwoman or a
modern-day fairy godmother. I had no idea that the phone
number could bring me one step closer to realising my
dream.

## CHAPTER 13

IT TOOK ME A FEW DAYS TO FIND THE COURAGE

to ring the number the lady had given me. Part of me was
excited and part of me thought that maybe he was a man
who needed the name of a good cobbler. I had learned not
to get my hopes up, but I was intrigued as to whose voice
would be on the other end of the phone.

Finally, I couldn't stand it any longer, so I picked up the
phone and dialled the number. After three rings it was
answered.

'Hello, VCA. David Kram's office.' VCA? He had a secre-
tary? I was momentarily relieved. At least I could find out
who he was without having direct contact with him and
making a complete fool of myself.

'Hello, my name's Peter Brocklehurst. I was given this
number to ring about singing. I'm a tenor.'

'Well, David is the person to talk to. He's the head
of opera at the VCA.' I was told to ring back later when
David would be available, so in the meantime I did some

homework and found out that I'd been given the number of the Victorian College of the Arts. They ran a postgraduate course for opera singers, and David Kram was the head of the opera department.

I knew I was kidding myself to think I could get into a post-university course; I had barely finished primary school. I really don't know what it was that made me ring again, maybe I just needed to hear from another expert about my voice and just wanted to know for sure whether or not I was fooling myself.

When I made the call, David himself answered. I decided to use the same tactics as when I'd rung Stephen Grant. I thought if I made myself sound really bad, then he might be just a little surprised when he met me. I knew I had to be careful though, for if I sounded too bad I wouldn't even get an audition. I couldn't believe it when he agreed to give me an audition, then I started thinking, *What have I done?*

Carol was still very supportive of my ambition, although by this stage our relationship was over. It seemed that we just had too many hurdles to overcome, too many unresolved issues from our pasts, and perhaps the relation-ship had been doomed from the start. We had moved to live on a farm in Warrnambool, but I was still trying to run the shop. The constant travelling back and forth from Melbourne to Warrnambool meant that we often only spent the weekends together. It was starting to feel as though the emotional distance between us was as great as the physical distance.

Even so, Carol reassured me that I was good enough, that I should go into the audition with my head held high and show them my stuff. Part of me was extremely scared. I think I kept expecting someone to tell me that I really was kidding myself and not to be so silly as to think I could ever sing opera. Although I had nothing to lose, in many ways I had everything to lose. While the dream remained just that, a dream, it was mine and no one could come along and take it from me. To expose the dream was to leave it open. To allow others in gave them the power to take the dream from me.

The day of my audition arrived and things couldn't have been worse. I'd had an abscess on a tooth for about a week and it hadn't cleared up, so I was in a lot of pain. I hadn't even been able to shave and found it hard to talk properly. I actually gave serious thought to not going at all, just giving up there and then.

So it was that I fronted up on the appointed day, nerves and excitement, fear and adrenalin coursing through my body. The VCA is right next to the National Gallery on St Kilda Road in Melbourne. The stately old red brick buildings of times gone by stand alongside newer, architect-designed structures, specifically built to enhance the acoustics for singers and musicians. The old and the new, tradition and the future, standing side by side.

I sat in the hallway of the opera building, feeling like a kid about to meet the school principal. I thought about my past and wondered what the future held for me. In a very short time I would know. Were my hopes just pipedreams after all, or could they become real?

Then it was time. I climbed the stairs to a small room and sitting inside was a piano and two men—my judge and jury.

'I'm David Kram, and this is Maestro Vladimir Vais,' one of them said. His smile didn't extend to his eyes as he shook my hand and I could tell that he thought I was wasting his time. He continued, 'What have you got?'

I looked at both these men and knew that it was now or never. I took a deep breath and told them, 'One long story and one song.'

I had been taking lessons from Stephen for about nine months, and had spent most of that time studying one aria called 'Che Gelida Manina'. I looked at David Kram who had moved to sit at the piano and told him the song. Then I walked to the piano and stood holding it. As he played the first note, I shut my eyes and disappeared into the music.

I knew I couldn't let myself think, now was not the time to worry about notes or technique. I just needed to go to that magical place inside of me, to let the song transform myself and my surroundings.

As the top C towards the end of the aria hung in the air I came back to reality. I slowly opened my eyes, ready to have my dreams shattered. I could barely finish the last lines. Staring straight at me, no more than a foot away, was the face of Vladimir Vais. The look on his face was one of shock and disbelief.

I could barely recognise David Kram as the same man who had greeted me. He no longer looked disinterested. He was staring up at me open-mouthed, and I was sure I could see a tear in his eye.

Maestro Vais was the first to speak. Still staring straight at me, in his thick Russian accent he said, '*Mein Gott*. A voice like that comes along once in a hundred years.' He said no more.

David Kram might have said something but I was too occupied with what Maestro Vais had said to allow anything else to sink in. All I remember was that I was enrolled almost on the spot. There and then, nearly thirty years since I had last been in a classroom, I became a student again.

The joy I felt at being accepted into the college was soon tempered by the reality of the situation I found myself in. But that day, when they listened to me sing and accepted me, I felt as if I were the luckiest man alive.

The classes I took were held in the evenings, so I arrived at the college as city workers were heading home. As I made my way along St Kilda Road, I passed the Arts Centre. And even though I was surrounded by people, some evenings I took the time to stop and look at the great spire and allowed myself to dream. *One day, maybe one day I'll be singing there.* I would have gone on my hands and knees and begged just to be allowed in the chorus.

Then I'd continue on to the Victorian College of the Arts. I'd turn up the path that led to the door with the School of Music sign. The corner where the path turned to the door was referred to as 'The Turn-in' by a few of the students, and every time I turned that corner, I felt I was turning towards my dream.

But dreams don't help much when you are trying to complete—and compete—in a world with its own rules and expectations. It wasn't long before I came to realise and accept the brutal truth that the strength of my voice alone was only part of what was needed. Whether it was that old nagging self-doubt or something else, I began to believe that I should not have thought the postgraduate course was the answer to my dreams.

Looking back, I wonder whether they really did me a favour by accepting me because it didn't take me long to feel like a stranger in a foreign land as I battled with the concepts of curricula, textbooks and lessons. Even the language used was alien to my world. Academia has a vocabulary all of its own, and unless you have come through the education system, trying to decipher even the most basic concept can become a nightmare. That sort of knowledge is taken for granted by those who had been taught—I thought a treble clef was a speech impediment.

We were also expected to read music, have a working knowledge of German and Italian grammar and know something of the history of drama and music. I didn't even understand English grammar. I felt like a man put into a swimming race when the other competitors had already competed ten laps, while I was left to dogpaddle down the shallow end. I don't know what I would have done had I not met a wonderful woman called Margaret Orr, who took me under her wing and helped me navigate my way through the first year.

Like me, Margaret was not fresh out of high school but, unlike me, she was very well educated. She has a beautiful soprano voice but family life had overtaken any career ambition she may have harboured. We found ourselves the odd ones out, surrounded by talented younger students. Margaret was kind and generous with her help and support, and our enduring friendship is one of the few positive things I took with me from the college.

As in any of the creative arts, the bottom of the ladder in opera is a very crowded place. And here again I found myself not really fitting in. I had been given special consideration when I was accepted on the strength of my voice alone, but that was where the consideration ended. I don't blame anyone at the college; I had been given a chance and was expected to catch up to the rest of the students in my own time. There was resentment among some students that I had got into the college at all, and a number of jealousies surfaced.

One thing I did learn is that any competitive field is rife with politics. The college was certainly competitive, as students vied for the best roles in productions. As the year wore on it became glaringly apparent that I didn't belong; I was totally out of my depth in an environment that was doing little or nothing to enhance my singing, only exposing me to the theory and academic structure of singing which I didn't understand anyway. All the effort and hardship I was putting myself through seemed to be for no real end.

The only thing I had going for me was my voice. The reality of my everyday existence told me I had a lot of things going against me. I can remember a mental conversation I had with myself where I stood at The Turn-in and wondered: *How am I ever going to be able to be an opera singer? I'm too old, I don't speak any languages and I can't read music.*

The drawbacks were even more apparent as I looked around and saw myself surrounded by those who highlighted what I wasn't. Kids who were beautiful, talented and well educated were fighting and scratching for minor roles in obscure opera companies.

I eventually had to admit the futility of trying so hard to belong in a place that I had no business being in and where I didn't want to be. The college and the course it runs just weren't for me. I had no ambition to perform a chorus role in a minor opera company. My dream had always been to sing classical songs to a concert audience and eventually play the lead role in an opera, so all the struggle was for an end that I didn't actually want. Having said that, I am proud that I managed to pass the first year.

Many factors contributed to my decision not to continue. My relationship with Carol had ended badly and, although she was still incredibly supportive of my singing, we knew before I'd even started the course that we could no longer be together. And financially things were a real struggle. I still had a family to support and singing lessons weren't part of the college curriculum so I had been financing those myself. The good times had come to an end with a crash.

The end of my relationship with Carol was utter torment. We both felt we couldn't live without each other, but together we destroyed each other. When we finally made the break it was almost like letting go of an addiction. For a while the good times had been so fantastic, they were worth staying for. But the good times became less and less and we found we were clinging to each other for all the wrong reasons, neither of us willing to let go.

Carol had brought out the best in me. Perhaps I was scared that without her, I would become a shell of a man. And for a while I think that's exactly what happened. When we finally parted, I was flat broke and had nowhere to live. I still had the business, but had been concentrating so hard on studying in my year at the VCA that I had let things slide. I lived for a short time in a Salvation Army hostel. We'd done so when I was a kid and the family had found itself stranded. But this time the smell of cigarettes, urine and old bodies was mingled with the sickly aroma of dope. It was a pungent, unforgettable mix and even after I left, the smell followed me everywhere, visiting my senses even today when I think of how bad life can be.

When I came out of the hostel I managed to pull myself together enough to return to the tiny room at the back of the shop and make it my home, such as it was. I lived in squalor, in keeping with the dreadful world I had built around me. When the horror of September 11 was played out on my portable TV, the self-pity that gnawed at my insides made me think only of the sick irony that it wasn't only my world that was coming to an end.

I began to feel it was better to live without hope. At least then you don't have to suffer the disappointments. Emotionally I was a wreck and I turned to some of the habits of the past to cope with the pain. Some mornings I would wake up wishing I hadn't.

I didn't let myself think about singing. I knew I couldn't go back to the band scene; I was too old for the whole rock-and-roll thing. And I was too uneducated to sing opera.

For once, instead of looking to find strength within my family I shut myself off from everyone I cared about. I deliberately avoided Sharon and the girls, not wanting them to see me. They say the higher you rise, the harder you fall. But maybe you have to hit rock bottom before you can find the strength to crawl back up again.

And one night, after I don't know how long, I woke with somebody's fingers down my throat. She held my head while I vomited semi-digested pills from my system. It seemed that I couldn't even escape properly, just enough to ensure I felt sick and sorry for myself as I recuperated in the back of the shop for the next few days.

I don't know the identity of my Florence Nightingale. She disappeared as quickly as she came. It turned out that she had been passing by the shop and noticed my legs sticking out from behind the counter. The front door had never shut properly and I thank God that it was one of those jobs I'd never got around to fixing. I don't know what would have happened if the kindness of a stranger hadn't intervened that night, but I did know that I had only two options.

One was to give up completely, which I had almost done. The other was to go on and see where life took me. Once again, at my lowest point I turned to God and somehow found the spiritual strength to keep going, to battle through the depression and see what the future held.

The first thing I had to do was leave the filth of the shop. I came to realise that I wasn't living in the shop, I was dying in there. I put a notice up in the window, 'Accommodation Wanted', and a man came in and told me about a room he and his wife had for rent above their garage.

As soon as I walked through the front gate into their garden I felt at home. A path lined with flowers took me to the rose garden in the backyard, and tucked away in the corner was a two-storey building with a garage on the ground floor. My new landlord unlocked the door and took me up the stairs to a room, complete with a kitchenette and a bedroom nook. Estate agents would describe it as a studio apartment; to me it became a nest where I could hide myself away in safety from the rest of the world.

For the first time in my life, I was creating a home on my own. I never considered the places I'd stayed after I left Sharon as permanent, and I'd only ever felt at home with other people around me. Now it was just me. At times the loneliness was awful, not having anyone to share my day, to laugh or even enjoy a meal with. I had a lot of time to think, and it was a time when I came to know myself. Not how I was seen through the eyes of others, but who I really was.

It took a long time, but I began to find happiness in things again—simple things. I began to sing, not for an audience, not for study, but for me, because I loved it and it made me feel whole. All those years ago in the orchards I had sung with the sun on my back and flies buzzing around when I was sure no one could hear me. In my new home and my little shop, my music became mine again and I sang—simply, purely and honestly—for the joy of it. It was my way of expressing what was deep in my heart and soul.

As I gradually became emotionally stronger, those old daydreams started to swirl around in my head again. My experience at college had taught me that I would never really make it as an opera singer, but still I harboured a flickering of ambition. I suppose it's like some people who dream of winning the lottery. The 'what ifs' pop into your head unbidden, almost as though to tease you.

I suppose anyone who has dreamt of a career in show business occasionally thinks of the stories about stars who have been discovered pumping petrol or waiting on tables. I hadn't heard of anyone being discovered in a shoe-repair shop. Then again, you never know unless you've tried.

Not long after I'd taken over the shop in Hawthorn, a man had come in who I recognised straight away as one of the superstars of Australian music, Graeham Goble. He had been a member of the Little River Band, one of the most successful Australian bands both here and internationally.

I couldn't believe this great man was actually standing in my shop. I still thought of those who had 'made it' as being in a different zone to the rest of us mere mortals, yet here he was, breathing the same air as me. He left me some shoes to fix, and when he came to pick them up I made my move, presenting him with a demo tape of rock songs I had put down with the band. This was quite a few years before I'd really started concentrating on opera and, although he took the tape, he never got back to me, which was a disappointment. In reality, of course, he was probably given all sorts of tapes by weirdos approaching him.

In spite of this, however, I still thought that one day it might happen, that one day someone would find me. I suppose when you have lived with a dream for most of your life, that dream takes a long time to die. And so, even though I had resigned myself to fixing shoes for the rest of my life, I still shared my dream occasionally with those who showed any interest.

Maybe it was a symptom of living alone and a way to combat the loneliness I felt, but I found myself talking to customers about my life. Perhaps the thoughts that filled my head needed to be verbalised to make them real and concrete. People have always told me that I talk too much, but I was to learn that sometimes it's not necessarily a bad thing.

One day a man walked in who needed a buckle on his sandals fixed, and he noticed a picture of my girls behind the counter. We began to chat and he seemed genuinely interested in my life. Try as I might, I couldn't fix that buckle, so over a period of about five weeks we got to know each other quite well. His name was Glenn Nicholson and he reminded me of a big grizzly bear. He was quite stocky with a bushy beard and a moustache.

I soon learned Glenn was the sort of man who thinks very carefully before he speaks, unlike me as I tend to chat away in a stream of consciousness. As the weeks went by, I began to sense there was more to Glenn's questions than idle curiosity. He would take a deep breath and then pause before probing further and deeper about my life. He gave me the name of Melbourne businessman and arts patron, Richard Pratt, and suggested I write him a letter outlining my ambitions.

I gave little thought to the suggestion, simply because while things weren't as bad as they had been, I'd had enough of knock-backs and false starts. I had no intention of putting myself on the line again, only to be kicked down. I was determined to find contentment fixing shoes.

When finally I managed to fix his buckle, I was actually a little disappointed as I knew that the friendship I was developing with this man would be over.

I was surprised when Glenn entered my shop again a few days later. At first I thought the buckle had broken again, but I soon learned he had another motive. After a few minutes of pleasantries, he let me know why he was there.

'I don't want you to write that letter any more,' he said. Maybe he'd known from the outset it would never have been sent, even if I'd written it, that I was emotionally in no position to rekindle my dreams.

Before I could say anything or confess my guilt at not following his advice, he continued. 'I've got a better idea,' he said. 'I'll introduce you to my brother-in-law.'

I don't know what I was expecting when I agreed to meet for a coffee with Glenn's brother-in-law. I knew he was interested in my singing ambitions and thought maybe his brother-in-law wanted me to sing at a function. The morning we arranged to meet, my curiosity was at bursting point. Glenn was playing his cards close to his chest. As I've said, he is a man of few words and is not one to make empty promises. I don't even think he knew what would come of the meeting.

When the phone rang that morning to tell me the appointment had been cancelled, the anger that welled up inside me was directed more towards myself than anybody else. I had stupidly allowed my hopes to be raised again and the daydreams to start. I had begun to imagine all sorts of ridiculous scenarios, and at one point I'd begun to question my sanity. Throughout all of the jolts I'd had, one thing I kept telling myself was that they were all part of a learning experience, that I would never leave myself open or vulnerable to be kicked down again. Yet here I was, fantasising that a meeting with a stranger would somehow change the course of my life.

Five times the meeting was cancelled. Trying to get the three of us together seemed an impossible task, so the sixth time I rang Glenn before he could ring me and told him not to bother any more. 'I'm sick of appointments being cancelled,' I told him. 'I can't do this—let's just forget it.' But I couldn't escape the feeling I was about to hang up on my last chance. The 'what ifs' surfaced in my head again, teasing me with uninvited and unanswered questions and the implausibility of my dreams. Dreams that had plagued me my whole life, making me want something that turned out to be just a fantasy.

Glenn's voice interrupted my thoughts as he said, 'We're on our way.'

I was soon to learn that even my wildest fantasies couldn't compete with reality.

My lack of enthusiasm must have been apparent to Nick when he walked into my shop. I looked up and saw a man wearing a baseball cap. He didn't look wealthy and I absently wondered what sort of shoes he needed fixing.

He was a solid man with a confronting stare, his bright blue eyes seeming to sum me up instantaneously.

Then he smiled and held out his hand. 'Peter? Peter Brocklehurst?' he asked. 'I'm Nick Columb. My brother-in-law, Glenn, has told me a little bit about you. He's parking the car. Let's go and get a coffee.'

His directness hit me between the eyes and all my resolve to forget the dream evaporated in the face of such bluntness. I immediately downed tools, turned the sign on the door around so that it read 'Closed' and walked—no, strutted— behind Nick and out the door.

The three of us went to the Geebung Polo Club in Hawthorn. Nick sat opposite me and said, 'Righto boy, tell me your story.' Coffee turned into lunch as I gave him an abbreviated version of my life. This was my first challenge with Nick, as anyone who knows me will testify that for me to abbreviate any story is quite an achievement. When I finally got to the end he looked across the table and I knew

I was being assessed. Then he spoke. 'What do you want to do with your life?' he asked.

I took a deep breath and began to reveal my dream to this man sitting opposite me. I knew I had to be as realistic and honest as possible with him. He was aware of my lack of education, so I told him that I not only needed singing lessons and a repertoire coach, but I had to learn to speak— or at least to sing—in Italian. When I'd finished, he shook my hand again and told me he would be in touch.

For the next few days, I had this inexplicable sense of apprehension and excitement. It was like a spring tightly coiled inside me. I had no idea what kind of impression I'd made, nor did I know what Nick's intentions were. Maybe he was going to try to convince me to return to college, or perhaps he was looking for someone to sing at a function after all?

I did sense that he was a man of great passion and deter-mination. My heart leapt every time the phone rang, only to plummet when a customer's voice asked when their shoes would be ready. Finally, when it seemed that yet again a cruel hoax had been played on me, I answered the phone and it was Nick.

'I just wanted to let you know that I haven't forgotten you.' His enthusiasm was infectious, even down the phone line, and I knew I would find it hard to keep a lid on the excitement as he continued. 'There's two ways I can do this,' he said. 'So I'll get back to you in a couple of days and let you know what's happening.'

I hung up the phone and stood as though in a trance. *Two ways I can do this.* He was going to do it! But what exactly was 'this' ? Whatever it was and whatever happened, it had to be an improvement on the life I was living at the time. *Two ways I can do this.* What on earth was he talking about? Whatever it was, something was definitely happening. Somehow and as faint as it might be, the dream was in my sights again.

The small seed of hope began to make its way to the surface. Now instead of banishing my daydreams to the back of my mind, I found myself staring into space, waiting for the phone to ring so that it might reveal my future. It was horrible and wonderful, scary and exciting all at the same time.

It was difficult to cope with and so I kept up an internal dialogue with myself. After all, I told myself, what Nick had said was only words; I had yet to see anything concrete. How many false promises had I believed before, only to have my hopes shattered? But then maybe, just maybe, this time it was real.

I went into a world of my own, only half-aware of what was going on around me, as I travelled from home to the shop and back again, resenting every phone call that wasn't from Nick, scared to spend too long in the shower in case he rang. What did he have in mind? Who was he talking to? When would he ring?

I had done a bit of my own homework and learned Nick was an extremely successful businessman and racehorse owner. This wasn't a man who had time to waste, and as the days wore on, I convinced myself he had more important things to do, that maybe he'd put me on the backburner, something to follow up on when it suited him.

I was putting the advertising sandwich-board on the footpath one morning when the phone rang. I knew it was

Nick. As I flew in the door to answer it, I hesitated. He would be apologising for raising my hopes. He had given it some thought and decided it wasn't for him. He had enough to do already and didn't have the time. He'd wish me luck for the future, and then that would be it.

All these thoughts tumbled around in my frantic mind so that, in the time it took me to run into the shop, I'd become angry with myself for allowing my hopes to be raised again. I was almost crying as I picked up the phone. My premonition was right. It was Nick.

'Peter,' he said with that unmistakable gruffness of his. 'Nick here. Job's right, I'm going to do it myself. Let's discuss it in detail over lunch.'

Are there actually times in a person's life when they know things will never be the same again? I can't say for certain that I stood in the shop that morning and knew that something momentous had happened. I can only reflect and I have to say that hindsight has become muddied by all that has occurred since then. But looking back, as I hung up the phone I knew with a conviction I could taste that my life was changed forever.

It was my moment and it was as pivotal and as critical as any I had ever experienced. And it became blindingly, brilliantly obvious that I would never again be the person I had been when I woke up that morning.

I wasn't yet a different person, but the journey to become a different me had begun.

## CHAPTER 14

## THOSE WITH AN EYE FOR A RACEHORSE

always consult an expert before buying a yearling. While I had been doing a bit of amateur sleuthing on Nick, he had also been checking out my credentials. After speaking to David Kram and Vladimir Vais from the college, and Stephen Grant, he had made his decision.

He told me later that originally he'd looked at bringing in business associates to invest in my future, but the whole process got too messy and confusing, so he decided to invest in me on his own. He was offering to finance my dream.

From the start of this incredible journey the one thing I have always been sure of is Nick's belief in me and my ability. As I've got to know him I've learned he is nobody's fool, so to have a man like that believe so passionately in me and my voice has given me a sense of self-belief that has been lacking all my life.

Of course, on that first day when we sat down to officially begin our new relationship I was plagued with doubts.

I could tell Nick believed in me, but did I really believe in myself? Life up until that point had taught me some very hard lessons, and I told myself the self-doubts that had been nurtured by decades of reinforcement would take a long time to leave me.

Then the other half of me, the seldom-heard optimist, said, *What have you got to lose?* I wasn't turning my back on anything to take this opportunity and I knew that should everything fail, I could always go back to shoe repairs.

I have never tried to analyse too deeply what it was about Nick that allowed me to trust him. My innate distrust of men had stayed with me, yet here I was, able to trust this man with my life, a man who had been a stranger just a few weeks ago. I did question his motives a few times in the beginning, but could come up with nothing other than his wanting to be involved with me in reaching my dream. And in reality, what could his ulterior motive be? He had a lot to lose and could ultimately gain nothing. I, on the other hand, had nothing to lose and could gain everything.

Nick asked me to sit down and work out all my debts, and estimate how much I thought it would cost me to live and study opera for a twelve-month period. Even this I found daunting; what if I asked for too much or too little? I'd thought I'd be studying part time while keeping the shop going, maybe employing somebody to run it when things got too busy. Nick had other ideas. Finally we settled on a scholarship sum, and within two weeks the shop that had been my life (and my occasional home) for so many years was closed.

It's hard to put into words what the next few weeks were like as my dream began to take shape. I felt slightly sentimental as I wound down the business. The little shop had operated from the same site for one hundred and thirteen years. I felt a sense of history being lost as stock was loaded into the back of my car to be stored in Sharon's garage. Generations of cobblers and boot-menders had worked here before me, and I felt a responsibility for their memories and spirit that had somehow been part of my working day.

Shortly after I left the shop it became an extension of the business in the building it was attached to. The façade was changed accordingly, so it was with dignity that this once thriving staple of the local community slipped into history.

One sunny afternoon in February 2002, Nick and Glen arrived at the shop with a bottle of French champagne and a friend of theirs, David Silver, with a video camera. Most of the customers had already collected their shoes, those who hadn't could do so around the corner at Siblings Restaurant.

We taped a crude sign saying 'Gone Singing' to the front door, popped the champagne and toasted the future. I think that's when it really hit me. This was actually real, my dream was happening. I could never have imagined that a stranger would one day walk into my shop and offer me the life I had always yearned for. All of the years of dreaming and hoping, of waiting for that miracle, and now it was actually happening.

Even today, when I am asked to describe what it felt like that morning, I shake my head and search in vain for the right words. Perhaps there are some things that cannot be put into words and to attempt to do so is to lessen the reality. Few people actually get to live their dream, to experience the thrill of living a fantasy. But that is exactly what I found myself doing.

Nick opened up his chequebook to me. He opened up his heart, and he and his beautiful wife Rosanne, together with their two little girls, Raphaela and Romany, have opened up their home. I'm sure at times it must seem to Rosanne that she has gained another family member. I know it does to Nick, and I certainly feel like one of the family. They opened up their lives, but most of all Nick opened up my dreams and belief in myself.

The transition from the old to the new was gentle and unhurried. My commitments consisted of singing lessons with Stephen, repertoire work with Vladimir who was more than happy to re-establish our relationship, and Italian lessons with a lovely woman called Carmen Ayres, a friend of Nick's. Margaret, who has been such a beautiful friend since college, generously gave up her time to teach me music theory, German and French.

I was to learn the extent of Nick's influence and contacts the morning of my first Italian lesson. As we sat drinking coffee at an outside table at a café just near Carmen's house, I noticed a familiar figure on the other side of the road. Not familiar in the sense of someone I knew, but someone I knew of. I was wondering if maybe he was an old customer from the shop when Nick suddenly gestured and called out.

'Mike! Mike!' he shouted. I stayed where I was as Nick raced across the road to speak with this man. I daren't go over and intrude, for by this stage I realised that he was talking to was Mike Brady.

It was some time after that I was to officially meet Mike

at a lunch organised by Nick. I'll never forget the moment that he introduced us.

'Mike Brady, I want you to meet one of the greatest tenor singers in the world, Peter Brocklehurst. Peter, this is Mike Brady.' I stood up from my seat in the restaurant and shook the hand of one of the most successful songwriters in Australia. There would be few Australians who haven't heard one of the 5000 jingles Mike has written, among them the 'Hard Yakka' and 'SPC Baked Beans & Spaghetti' songs. Of course, he will always be known for those brilliant football anthems 'Up There Cazaly' and 'One Day in September' as well as the many serious works he has composed. Suddenly it hit me. The door had opened and I had been allowed in. I was now part of that other zone, that place where the stars breathed the air and knew each other by first names.

I found a church in Hawthorn that was more than happy to allow Vladimir and me to rehearse there every Monday and Wednesday. Nick responded to their generosity by donating to their parish. The strongest feeling I had the first time we practised was humility as my voice echoed around that beautiful building, accompanied by Vladimir on piano. In the next few months I became accustomed to singing for a select group of people. I knew Nick moved in circles I had only ever dreamed of and he was slowly charting a course for my future success. I was introduced to people in the media, television and music business.

But those first few months were a difficult time for me, physically and for a variety of reasons. I had only really given away the smokes for good just a few months earlier. All those years of shoe repairs had exposed me to countless glues and solvents, so how much poison my system ingested over the years was anybody's guess. But once I was living a healthy life it was as if my body decided to cleanse itself. In those early days I seemed to have a perpetual cold or sore throat and I'm sure at times Nick must have felt that he'd invested in a brumby rather than a thoroughbred.

The lingering memory of my throat operation, and a sense of duty to Nick, finally sent me to visit a doctor for a complete check-up. As I sat in his waiting room I felt as if I were tempting fate. If something was wrong I really didn't want to know. I wanted the dream to last just a little bit longer.

The scars from the operation to remove the nodules were still evident, but amazingly I was given a clean bill of health. While many of the world's great singers have had their voices nurtured—almost wrapped in cotton wool—I'd abused mine to the point of destruction. The doctor confirmed what I'd suspected, my body was at last free to expel all the muck I'd exposed it to for so long. All those years of singing rock and roll, sometimes in shocking conditions and surroundings, came back at me, but not once, when Nick would bring people to hear me sing, did I hit a wrong note, no matter how sick I felt. I still knew how to put on a show and, if nothing else, it taught me that little in life is a waste, that most experiences count for something.

As an added bonus, for the first time in my life I was able to sit back and savour the world around me. I had always been so busy juggling work, singing and family commitments that I had never had the time to stop and smell the roses. I was committed to lessons for eight hours of the week; the rest of the time was my own. I began an exercise regime, walking in the mornings before spending most of the day reciting Italian, or practising my singing. And I ate well.

I had never built up good study habits, so I had to find my own way of committing my new knowledge to memory. Carmen would give me a phrase to learn, and I would recite it over and over again, almost like a meditation mantra, until it was committed to memory. I thought of it as swallowing words until they were digested by my mind. In the early days I did little else. I couldn't watch TV or read as all my concentration and energy had to go into memorising words.

At times it felt—and still does—as though I was learning two languages, for music is a language all of its own. The squiggles and lines on a page all mean something and learning and understanding them has been as difficult for me as getting my tongue around Italian.

Rather than sit alone all day in my little flat, I walked to local cafés, sat and—on the surface at least—watched the world pass by. I may have looked like a man of leisure as I sat with my latte, but inside I was working, mentally reciting new words and phrases, hoping they would stay with me. Just near the church where I was rehearsing is a particular café called Bacio Dolce, and this was where I would sit and learn Italian from the menu while I ate.

That was another change I had to adjust to. My whole working life had been physical, working with my hands. I would never have considered drinking coffee and using my mind as *real* work. My hands were now still, yet the work I was doing was harder than anything I had ever undertaken.

I was also moving in different circles and found it difficult at first to find my feet and know where I belonged.

Rubbing shoulders with the wealthy and elite of society was beyond comprehension in the world I had come from. These were people who were featured in society columns and who met at race meetings to discuss business deals. I became very self-aware, at times even self-conscious, as I engaged in conversation with people who seemed to be from another world.

As the months wore on, however, I noticed that I was beginning to relax in the company of Nick's friends and associates. I don't think it was that I had changed all that much, it was more that I came to realise those differences I had thought everyone else was so aware of were really only apparent to me. It was actually me who was judging myself. In a kind of reverse snobbery I was attributing my pre-conceptions and insecurities to those I met.

It was almost like travelling to a new country. At first you notice all the differences in those around you, but as time goes on you realise people have a lot more in common than you think.

Naturally, I couldn't have had a better guide than Nick as I navigated this new world. From the first time we met, he had never stopped dispelling the myths many people hold about those with wealth and power. He certainly didn't display the trappings of his life, usually looking less well off than I did. Yet he conveyed a sense of authority that drew people to him.

I soon came to realise that he and I had both entered a new world. Nick knew nothing about the music business when we started, but he made it his business to learn. He is not the sort of man who is content to let others tell him what's right and wrong. He certainly encourages opinions and listens intently to experts. Then he finds out for himself what works best.

He has made sure we have been advised by experts every step we've made. He consults with and defers to what I think of as 'vets'—people he checks facts with, who let him know whether or not he's on the right course. Whenever people approach him with an idea or suggestion, he will make a few phone calls to verify their credentials, and only then will he proceed any further.

It has become even more glaringly apparent to me than it was when I cut that first 45-inch vinyl in Warrnambool that the music business is just that, a business. Even the most talented singer in the world would find it hard to make it without some knowledge of business. And that is where Nick's expertise has been invaluable. He can wheel and deal with anyone and open doors that would have forever remained shut if it was just me knocking.

Among the greatest challenges for me since meeting Nick has been the change in my identity. If other people are to see me as a singer, that is how I must see myself. That has been part of the process I've gone through, reassessing many of my long-held habits and beliefs. Simple things, like considering rehearsals as work, have slowly contributed to the new persona I have developed. It is not a process that can be rushed or forced. Instead and over time, it has evolved naturally. And as I try to graft the new world to the one I was once a part of, I know I have to leave behind much of the old.

It has been in many ways a rebirth; a magnificent new start that promises so much. But it has also been a defining point in my life, in that in order to move forward I've had to ask what it was that brought me to this point. I've had to cope with and find a balance between the anguish and the anticipations, the memories and the hopes.

And at times it was all the more daunting because while the excitement of what might happen was something I had never felt before, I also couldn't help looking back at the countless times when my hopes had been raised, when there had been a glimmer of a chance that I might make it, when I had told myself that this time things will work out—only to have those dreams shattered.

Alone in my flat, shut away from the rest of the world, I sometimes thought of those times when it seemed so much easier to live without dreams.

As always, though, whenever I had down times I would turn to music for solace. So while practising songs was work, it was also the familiar comfort zone I used to keep me positive and focused on the goal Nick and I had set.

I was also surrounded by really positive support people. From the first time I'd met Vladimir at the VCA, he had reassured me with the words, 'I will help you, I will help you.' And he was true to his word. Always with me musically and spiritually, whether it be in the emptiness of the church in Hawthorn or on the stage at Crown Casino in Melbourne, Vladimir has been there.

About six months after we began, Nick and his close Sydney friends, John and Kris Messara, hatched a plot to 'sting' one of their great friends, Sydney radio personality Alan Jones. Vladimir and I were invited to a dinner at Nick's house and he told us he had also invited Alan who had flown down to Melbourne from Sydney for some radio awards.

I was very nervous as I got myself ready that evening. I was getting used to meeting the rich and powerful around Nick, but I knew this night had taken on a special importance in the plans he had for me. I was also worried that the 'sting' might backfire. For it to work, I had to really pull out all stops and impress this man.

Of course I had heard of Alan Jones. I knew he was a man of strong opinions and influence. I kept telling myself not to be intimidated by him and kept reminding myself that one thing I had re-learned over the past few months was not to pre-judge people, to wait until I had met them. A lesson I had learned quite early in life was reinforced, and I started to take people as I found them, not as they appeared to the public.

Nick had told me before the dinner not to talk too much; he didn't want to ruin the element of surprise. He sat me on the same side of the table as Alan, so conversation with him was fairly limited during dinner. I'm sure Alan must have been curious as to who I was, but he was too polite to ask what I was doing there. Vladimir, with his Russian accent, was assumed to be someone to do with the international racing industry. But at one stage Vladimir almost gave the game away. Between courses, Nick asked Vladimir if he wanted to play a bit of piano. When Alan was asked did he have any requests, he replied, 'Yeah, Rachmaninov.' Of course Vladimir proceeded to play a flawless array of pieces by the great man.

When finally coffee was served, it was time for Nick to show his hand. The conversation turned to music and Nick asked Vladimir to play some more on the piano.

'Does anyone here know how to sing?' asked Nick.

I piped up and said, 'I'll have a go.'

I stood next to the piano and looked over at Vladimir sitting at the keyboard, smiling.

'Maestro,' I said in the traditional way of asking if he was ready. He nodded slightly and, as Vladimir looked up, I noticed an oddly quizzical look come across Alan's face. Suddenly the thought struck me that, having discovered our deception, he'd be annoyed.

But there was no time to worry about that as Vladimir launched into a rendition of 'Musica Proibita' by Gastaldon. The music filled the room and I'd hardly finished the first stanza when I looked across to gauge the reaction. Alan was sitting quite still, the glass of wine in his hand untouched. He was literally open-mouthed and later told me that 'gob-smacked' best summed up how he felt. I then proceeded to sing the aria 'E' Lucevan Le Stelle' from Puccini's *Tosca*, which I was to find out later was coincidentally one of Alan's favourite pieces.

A night that had begun with such trepidation ended up being one of the most memorable of my life, and for all who attended. Many a duet and song was sung that evening. And it was the early hours of the morning before we finally finished singing around the piano. Alan could not have been more effusive. And as we chatted in between the songs, he continued to press me for details of my life and seemed genuinely interested in me and the journey I had taken.

From that night on my career began to snowball. Everyone we met seemed to get caught up in the enthusiasm generated by Nick, and opportunities came flooding in.

A good mate of Nick's, Bob Grieve, had connections with the producers of the ABC TV show *Australian Story*.

The ABC approached Nick to see if we were interested in them screening the story of my life. Believe it or not, we actually gave a lot of thought about whether or not to participate. Nick didn't want to hurry the process, and we were a little concerned the exposure might be too soon in my career. The timing had to be just right.

But finally we decided the potential of an Australia-wide audience was just what was needed to give my profile an extra lift. It was an enormous challenge to be so open and intimate in front of a television audience. Although I can seem very much an extrovert and I have no problems chatting to people about my life, in other ways I am very protective of my privacy.

Living alone meant I had created a world where it was just me, and not having the shop meant I could spend many days on end talking only to those I chose to speak to. So it was a little confronting to suddenly have a film crew following me around all day.

While all this was going on, Alan Jones invited me to sing at his Christmas party at Star City Casino in Sydney. This was an opportunity I couldn't pass up, but I was extremely nervous as the day approached.

We had to fly up and back on 16 December 2002. It was my first trip on a plane since we had arrived from England all those years ago to start the great adventure that had been my childhood. And here I was, at the start of another great adventure, again looking at an airplane, amazed it would ever get off the ground.

That feeling of being a child again stayed with me throughout the day. It was a magical experience. The room was filled with a who's who of Australian society and I was introduced to them as one of the greatest tenors in the world. And I don't mind admitting I was like a star-struck kid, as later I shook hands with people like Kieran Perkins and Brett Lee. One of the most special moments for me was when I asked Steve Waugh for his autograph. He shook my hand and laughed, 'Mate, it's me who should be getting your autograph.'

I had to take a deep breath and mentally pinch myself. I was here—these people were shaking my hand and congratulating *me*. Probably for the first time in my life, I felt I was good enough; I was comfortable in my own skin, talking to people who made me feel welcome. That night I began to feel that I belonged.

I can't overstate how important that sense of belonging was—is—to me. Throughout my life, I had always been different, always marked out as not really belonging and perhaps a little strange. School, work, play and even in the bands—none of them was a place where had I truly fitted in, let alone been one of the boys.

This desire of mine to sing classically had caused me so much grief over the years. But I had never let it go, never given it up in order to fit into a world where I felt excluded. Now that desire had brought me here to a place where I was being me. And I was being accepted, even applauded, for being who I truly was.

Later, sitting alone in my little flat, I allowed myself to go over the day of the Christmas party, savouring every conversation, not wanting to forget a single moment. And I realised that even though I was now more alone than I'd ever been in my life, I no longer felt lonely. I was beginning to find within myself the strength to face the challenges that lay ahead by looking back on the journey that had brought me to this point. For the first time in my life, I was truly happy with myself as a person; I was being who I was meant to be.

A lot of the self-reflection I went through came as a result of doing the *Australian Story* program. It was there that I had to go back over the events in my life—the constant travelling, the abduction and the failed relationships—and assess how they had brought me to this point. It's a strange thing to see your life condensed into half an hour for a television show. But at the same time the whole experience of being part of the program has been critical for a number of reasons.

A lunch was organised with Mike Brady, Nick, Bob Grieve and me to discuss a couple of issues, one of which was to ask Mike if he would co-write a song for me with Vladimir.

While Mike and Vladimir were working on the song, Mike very generously asked me if I would like to perform it at the Ron Barassi tribute dinner. This was just what we needed. It was also a chance for me to fulfil yet another of those hidden ambitions, to sing for a huge audience in a large stadium setting.

How many times had I driven past those stadiums and dreamed of one day performing there? It was of course one of those foolish wishes, something I could indulge in because I knew it would never come true. Yet here I was, only the third time I had even been in a stadium, and I was actually performing.

Was I nervous? Too right I was! Quiveringly nervous, to be precise. This wasn't the cosy, welcoming environment of the Christmas party. It wasn't singing for a select group of people in the church at Hawthorn. And it wasn't performing rock and roll for drunken crowds on a Friday night.

The Telstra Dome had been decked out especially for the night and the song Mike and Vladimir had written for me was called 'Credere', or in English, 'Believe'. It was a fantastic song and, naturally, I felt a great sense of pride and humility that it had actually been created for me. But beneath the bubbling excitement there were worries, not so much about my ability but more to do with the newness of where I was.

For the first time, for example, I was to perform with a full choir. Not only did rehearsals take an unreal quality, they instilled in me the joy of being supported by those who had dedicated their lives to the music I loved—alongside the dread that I might let them down. And being in such a huge place with such a massive audience had me worrying about the sound quality.

Backstage that night I could hardly keep the water down as I sipped nervously from my drink bottle, trying to quench my parched mouth. The film crew was still following me around, so I knew that if I did muck up, it would be broadcast to the nation.

Then, following Eddie Maguire's introduction, all that was left was me. It was me standing on the stage with nothing but the music—my music—between me and all those people. Then, as I prepared to sing, I glanced back at the awesome sight of the choir. The dread returned, more so. And yet, just as much part of the mix was the humility and unreal exhilaration at the fact that each of them would use their talent and their innate sense of loyalty to music so that they could give their full and unequivocal support to me and what I have to offer.

I took a deep breath and began. The music, the song, the choir and me, seemed to become one, and I felt all the insecurities melt away. The thumping nerves that had threatened to paralyse me vanished, replaced with an all-consuming passion as I lost myself to the song.

It's at times like this that I allow myself to live the dream, to believe in my new reality. My voice fills the auditorium; I am at last doing what I truly believe I was put on the earth to do. The need, the desire to be who I am, burns within me stronger than ever because this time it is real.

The adrenalin rush you get when you perform is unlike any other experience. The nerves, excitement and passion all come together to lift you to an indescribable high. I had felt this to a certain extent when I was in the rock and roll bands, but that was nothing like the intensity that comes with love, with the oneness of being the singer and intertwining what you are with what you have.

I must have needed something tangible to remind me of that night because when I came off stage I walked to one of the goal posts at the end of the ground and plucked out a small tuft of grass from the base. Among the many mementos I have collected since this incredible journey began, that tuft of grass, now dried and brown, reminds me of how I felt that night.

*Australian Story* was aired on 28 April 2003, and the response we got to the show can only be described as amazing. One thing that stood out was that those closest to me showed they were concerned the changes in my life might be too overwhelming and that perhaps I won't cope with so much so soon. But I tell myself I can manage. My ability to adapt to new surroundings and new situations is something that has developed by necessity in me over the years.

Throughout my life, ever since I was a little boy, the one thing that has always remained constant is change.

CHAPTER 15

IT IS NOW LATE 2003

and less than a year since *Australian Story* was shown on the
ABC, yet at times it feels like a lifetime ago. Incredible things
began to happen almost straight away. A few days after
it aired, Mike Brady received a phone call from a very
well-known and respected songwriter, asking if I would be
interested in recording one of his songs. When my phone
rang, at first I couldn't believe who I was speaking to. It was
Graeham Goble, the man I had given my demo tape to all
those years before when I was just a cobbler with a dream.
Now he was contacting *me*, offering me the chance to sing
one of his songs.

Doors that had been locked my whole life began to
open for me. Nick was fielding offers from record companies and tour promoters, and it seemed that everyone
wanted to become a part of the journey my life was taking.
Again Nick's business acumen came to the fore. He knew
this was not a process to be hurried and although the level

of interest was intense, he decided we should bide our time and involve ourselves only with the best.

At the risk of sounding repetitious, I say again that Nick's importance to me and to the course of my life has been remarkable. Not only has he been instrumental in setting the whole chain of events in action, he has continued to drive things once it all got going. It would have been easy for me to get caught up in the hype that was beginning to surround me, but one thing Nick has taught me is that it's easy to make empty promises. He knows when he is being fed a line, and he knows who is genuine.

Nick is a man of contradictions. Along with his astute business mind, he has great passion, and I count my lucky stars that he chose to direct that passion towards me and my career. He is stubborn and dogged. His need to control things means that when he doesn't understand something, he will make it his business to find out. What I've learned through Nick is that power needn't be abused by those who possess it. Nick uses influence, not manipulation, to achieve the goals he has set. He puts his heart and soul into whatever he does. He lies awake at night thinking about promotional ideas or plans. He is not happy unless his diary is full and his day is busy.

That he came into my life when he did is more than a dream come true. I needed someone with drive and ambition, as these traits either were not there or had been all but kicked out of me over the years. And, perhaps even given greater than this, and the financial security, there has been, for the first time in my life, a sense of emotional security. I have someone I can rely on and talk to when things get rough, when confusion and doubts set in, when nothing really makes sense

Whether by example or an innate generosity, Nick has endowed me with the confidence to believe in myself, the opportunity to express my deepest passion. Previously, the absence of expression, the constant yet unfulfilled desire within me had its impact on many other aspects of my life. I overreacted in and to so many situations simply because I had all these seemingly unrealistic desires bottled up inside me. The intensity of what was wrong with my life was exaggerated because I wasn't doing the one thing I knew I should be doing—singing.

Now I see there is much about this journey that I had never considered—never dared to think about—in the wildest daydreams of my yesterdays. There are, for example, people to do all sorts of things: producers, directors, sound technicians, experts on taxation, copyright, publishing, promotions—the list is endless. Then of course there is the legal side where, as well as everything else, the jargon of contracts is a language of its own.

So time and again I tell myself talent is not nearly enough and, if I'd had to deal with all of it on my own, I would have given up long ago, taken up the fags and driven around Australia again. It is truly frightening what can confront you and I no longer wonder how people in this business end up on the rocks or dead. Someone strong needs to make the hard decisions.

I've seen people come up to Nick and say, 'What the hell do you know about the music industry?' He is always honest and direct with his reply.

'I know nothing at all,' he says with a smile, 'but I know enough to get the right people who do know what they're talking about.'

I've watched him with people and marvelled at the ease with which he glides into a conversation and, almost immediately, arouses people's interest. They might not always like him, but they respect him.

So it goes without saying that the person I have become since this whole thing started has much to do with Nick. No, he has never actually sat me down and given me lessons, but there is a magnetism about him that makes it easy to listen and learn. I could not have asked for a better mentor as I entered this strange new world.

For a long time things felt surreal, unreal, like a reel of cotton spinning wildly. Although things were introduced slowly, the steps I was taking were huge. Looking back, I can see how far I've come in a very short time.

The unreality of it all hit home the day in August 2003 when we flew to Sydney to sign a recording contract with Sony. As we stood outside their Australian headquarters I took a moment to stand and look at the huge sliding doors leading to their offices. Less than twelve months before I would not even have dreamed of flying to Sydney, let alone of standing there about to sign a recording contract. With Nick by my side, we walked to the doors and they opened. The security guard checked his list of names and showed us in. As the doors closed behind us, I knew. We were in. I was in.

It turned out to be a day full of contradictions. First, I was welcomed to Sony like a family member; someone that day actually said, 'Welcome to the Sony family.' And in a way that's what it felt like. The offices were massive and yet I felt completely at ease and at home.

Then came the formality of signing on the dotted line.

I was worried my hand would shake too much but surprisingly there was a calmness in me, a calmness that was reinforced when I looked at the gold pen they'd given me for the signing and saw it had my name on it. I looked across at Alan Jones, his quiet smile reassuring me that I belonged. This was where I was meant to be.

Then they sat me down at a huge conference table with about twelve people who were all there to market and promote me. For a time I was discussed as a commodity, something to be marketed and packaged for the consumption of the general public. I won't say that I was bewildered, perhaps overwhelmed is an appropriate word. But, as much as I felt like a product, the thought didn't worry me. I smiled inwardly as they spilled out words like 'strategies', 'demographics' and 'target markets'. That was their world after all. And I felt safe because sitting right beside me in this room full of executives and publicists was Nick. I think he sensed my anticipation because he turned his head, nodded and then, reaching across grabbed my arm firmly as if to say, 'We're there, son. We're there.'

That old truism, nothing in this life is wasted, came back to me the day I started to record my CD. With a full orchestra behind me, I had to summon up all the professionalism I had relied on in the pub bands over the years so that I could perform. Now wasn't the time to feel nervous at what was happening. Now was the time to be as good as I possibly could be.

Even so, I felt a lump in my throat at the familiar tunes that echoed around the studio, waiting for my voice to bring them to life. What was especially difficult, though, was the song 'Because'. As I sang it my mind went back to all of those hundreds of places that made up my childhood: hearing Dad's sweet voice as he sang words of love to Mum; the day he brought the gramophone player to our home in Darwin and put that strange thing called a record on the turntable; our fishing and hunting trips out in the bush; the night I sang 'Amazing Grace' to all those people in Warrnambool.

But most of all it was the memories of Dad and Mum, him kneeling at her side with her sitting and smiling, softly telling her of his love through the songs he sang. That was the image that brought the stinging sensation to my eyes as I sang that beautiful song, thanking God the orchestra was positioned in another room so they couldn't see my tears.

Margaret's unwavering support for me became evident on a professional level, not only with her teaching, but now with her beautiful soprano voice as she joined me in a duet for the CD.

Nick has a saying: If a person has a yearling in the front paddock, all is well with the world—or something along those lines. Basically, it means that when there is hope for the future, bad times can be overcome. Perhaps that is why I am able to look back on the past at this point in my life. Memories and experiences previously too painful to recount no longer fill me with dread.

Who is the person the audience sees when I am standing on the stage? It is a question I have tried to answer. As I stand on the threshold of a new life, I have found the strength to look back.

Part of the journey has been the reflection of the past. It has been a process rather like putting together a jigsaw puzzle that has been left lying in pieces for years. Some of the pieces are more faded than others, and some might be in the wrong place, but they all belong; all have made me who I am today.

The first time we met, Nick carried a folder where he stored all the information that was relevant to our project. The folder is rather battered now, but Nick still carries it with him to meetings. On the front he has written, 'Work in Progress'. Perhaps one day the words will read, 'Completed Work'.

As I take the time to look back, I can recognise a certain pattern, a kind of interweaving symmetry, to the course my life has taken. Contemplating yet another trip interstate, I am reminded again of the small boy who stood on the tarmac in England, staring in fear at the aeroplane that was to take him to another life, a new world. It became a world where the journey seemed never-ending. It's rather odd that all these years later, Qantas has used the *Australian Story* episode about me as in-flight entertainment.

So it continues today. The constant travelling inter-state, only now the dodgy old cars and camping by the roadside have gone, replaced by business-class flights and accommodation in the best hotels; the confusions and frustrations of childhood eclipsed by a reassuring certainty. The journey might not be over yet, but I know where I am going. I have a clear destination in mind, so it is time for me to enjoy the ride.

At the time of writing, my CD has been number one in the classical charts for three weeks; I'm the first Australian artist to have had a number one classical hit for six years. I actually receive fan mail, and have been greatly moved by the genuine support and kind messages from those who I have touched with my voice. People call me 'Mister' when we meet. I sign autographs and do media interviews.

World-renowned tenor José Carreras agreed happily to meet with me. When Sony organised this meeting I was stunned to learn that Mr Carreras had heard of me. He held my CD in his hand, and we exchanged autographs before saying goodbye. I spent over twenty minutes with the great man; it is a meeting I'll never forget.

Part of my ambition is to bring the 'stuffy' world of opera into the modern day and to the younger generation. It became increasingly obvious early that I was achieving my goal as I witnessed the responses of my three beautiful daughters Sally, Cathy and Lisa. Three talented girls who are forging their own careers in the world of modern music. They regularly refer to me as their 'cool' dad; it is with pride that they introduce me to their friends and peers. It is a wonderful compliment to be referred to as cool by these young people.

Finally I am being the person I was put on this earth to be. I am a classical tenor singer.

The journey is certainly not over. But maybe now I can stop asking, 'Are we there yet?'

Since the time of writing I have fulfilled one of the biggest dreams of life: I performed to a full house in the concert hall at the Sydney Opera House in May 2004. What an amazing experience, made all the more magnificent because I was accompanied on stage by my beautiful friend, Australia's latest soprano, Margaret Orr. Also sharing the moment, with baton in hand, was the world-renown maestro, Vladimir

Vais, conducting the brilliant Opera Australia Orchestra.

It is every singer's wildest ambition to achieve a standing ovation in such a venue and I'm thrilled to say that I had this experience after I sang my final encore, 'Nessun Dorma'. This performance was a culmination of an amazing year, which started for me with the release of my first CD, *Boots and All*, debuting at number one on the national classical charts, achieving yet another dream.

To the wonderful people who have been touched by my music, bought my CDs and have made each live performance so memorable, I sincerely thank you for allowing me to live my dream. You are amazing.

# ACKNOWLEDGEMENTS

An acknowledgement section. Wow! Where am I to begin this mammoth task? I think I would like to start with the people at this end of my journey thus far. They say you can only thank someone so much before it becomes overdone. But I don't believe this is the case with regards to Nick Columb. 'Thank you.' Are they the right words? From the bottom of my heart—that is the right place—for everything!

If I had to pick but a few of the many things that you have given me, they would certainly be direction, advice, caring, and showing stubborn blind faith in me as a man, a singer and an 'adopted' member of your family. Though at times I have wanted to put my hands around your stubborn neck and shake the hell out of you, mostly I've wanted to put my arms around your big shoulders and embrace one hell of a human being who has shown unwavering confidence in the project that is my future, the project that is me.

You carry around with you a folder that contains documents relating to the project and on the cover it reads, 'Work in Progress'—and how far we have come. So from this 'work in progress', a toast to the man whom I call my best mate. Here's to you, Nick.

Rosanne Michie. You're so lovely and supportive. I know at times you must have felt as if you'd lost your husband to the project, but you hung in there. You put your best foot forward and have put up with so much, yet have still been such an amazing support. Thank you so much for all of your help, little lady.

Raphaela and Romany, thanks for keeping me in line, my little darlings. Thanks, Oscar, for your kind words.

Glenn Nicholson. How do I find the words to describe how I feel about you and your amazing insight, belief and support? How does 'You're the best banana' sound? An exciting prospect indeed is the thought of meeting the rest of your family if the first introduction is anything to go by. Thank goodness for wonky sandals. Go Wolfman!

Vladimir Vais. You are my guru. Your belief in me and my potential is the ultimate. It's scary stuff. Your credentials and the support of your lovely wife, Val, are the only two things that speak louder. The guidance and love from both yourself and Val is just daunting. My love to you both.

Carmen Ayres. You started out as my Italian coach. You ended up being a faithful friend. Just to know you are around is tonic enough to sustain me when I am low. You're amazing. Thanks for the strength and encouragement. *Grazie*.

Stephen Grant. From the start you have believed in me

and guided me vocally. Your friendship cannot be under-stated. What a fantastic voice teacher and friend.

At the beginning of this musical odyssey, I was stunned to find just how great is the quality of treasures that exist on this earth, when Nick introduced me to John and Kris Messara. Your influence in this project has been integral. You and your beautiful family are an absolute godsend. What a thrill to say I have such friends.

Through Kris and John, I was introduced to my relent-less friend Alan Jones, one of my biggest supporters. What a hard-working, charitable, big-hearted, selfless gentleman. Australia is a lucky country and those who know you and what drives you would testify that whoever coined that phrase must have known we would be blessed by you and your amazing spirit.

There are so many more wonderful people who have had a positive effect on my journey such as Brigid Donovan, Bob Grieve, David Silver, John Sinclair, Hugh Halliday, Mike Brady (thanks mate), Graeham Goble, Mickie Braithwaite, Jim—my first Italian lesson (*bacio dolce*—keep the lattes coming, mate). Also thanks to Dr David Kram, Blair Edgar, Helen Noonan, Irina Cherkassky, Phillipa Sasey and Mattia Mercurio. A very special thanks to Larissa Oberfeld. Heart-felt thanks to all of you.

My Sony family. Denis Handlin, Chris Bent, Cathrine Mahoney and Cassandra Tenant-Pascoe and everybody who has worked tirelessly on my album.

Thanks also to the staff at Allen & Unwin, particularly to Jo Paul, whose commitment and enthusiasm have made this project possible.

Evelyn Klopfer—my lovely friend in Sydney who has

been an inspiration. Thank you for working tirelessly for my benefit. I would be lost without you. Willie Cull, the first fan to make me feel like a star. Your smiles and warmth are indeed a ray of sunshine. Indeed, my thanks to all the wonderful people who sent cards and letters since *Australian Story* aired. And Rita (Mini the Mermaid), my Northern Princess, where would I be without your friendship?

Thanks also to Doreen and Jim Carolyn for looking after me.

Before this magic began, I was at the crossroads of my turbulent life and could not have arrived at the starting blocks without the strength and encouragement of my lovely family and friends. Mum and Dad (Tom and Helen), thanks for the love. And to Paul, Mandy, Josie, Sarah, Jamie, Tommy and Becky—all my wonderful sisters and brothers who kept popping up. (Whew. Mum and Dad, they say it keeps happening until you find out what causes it. I guess you worked it out!) Thanks also to their wonderful partners, Christine, Tom (a special mention—thanks, mate), Fred and Colin, and also Wendy. Also a very special mention to my friend Anita O'Donnell (deceased) and Victor Ellis.

To my Nan and granddad (both deceased) who taught me so much about life.

My special friends, Ronnie, Bernard, Joe Willis, Peter (Prof) Walters, Peter Bird, Damien Webster (keep slapping the cat) and Melville Proud (one in a million), Carol Reid and last but not least Mark and Sally-Anne, my sibling friends and latte and Thai beef specialists. FMUDA. A huge thanks and appreciation for the friendship and help from my buddies Alan and Michelle Cook and their two little cherubs. Love from Uncle Funny Peter.

Margaret Orr. What a wonderful jewel uncovered when first you sang in your amazing soprano voice for me. We began our classical journey at the same time as you offered your love, friendship and support. One of the highlights of our journey was your splendid two-take effort in our duet on *Boots and All*. Unwell and inexperienced, you exceeded everybody's expectations. What a gift, what an experience, what a magical lady. Thank you for carrying me through my year at the VCA, my little friend.

Importantly, to a special person, a lady who has success-fully mothered our three beautiful daughters so lovingly and unselfishly. Sharon, the years of tireless devotion that you gave me and our girls cannot be equalled. We grew up together and though we may have grown apart in many ways, and eventually drifted apart, my respect, love and admiration will always be rock solid. You're the best and our girls Sally, Cathy and Lisa (Dooby) are glowing testament to your absolute love and care. Shine on, Shadow.

Sally, my mate. You have been and will continue to be an inspiration to me and all who cross your beautiful path. What an absolute lady. Keep your happiness, your glowing smile, work hard on your golden voice and look out world!

Cathy, you gorgeous baby. Your smile is enough to cause anyone's heart to skip a beat, to say the least, for your amazing talent.

Lisa, you broke my heart when you were born and now it seems, like your sisters, you are destined to break many more with your stunning looks and soaring talent.

I love you all so much and am so very proud to call you my daughters.

*Peter Brocklehurst*

*peter*BROCKLEHURST

BOOTS*and*ALL

Peter Brocklehurst's debut album, *Boots and All*, is available now. As we go to print, Peter is in the studio recording his second album.